Advance Praise for
The Pledge to America

"I had the honor of serving with Drago Dzieran in combat. He exemplified everything a warrior should be: smart, courageous, aggressive, disciplined, determined, strong, loyal, and patriotic. I knew he would never let me down. This book, detailing Drago's incredible life, provides a detailed insight into the heart of this warrior—and offers an inspiring story for every American."
— JOCKO WILLINK, US Navy SEAL LCDR (Ret),
    Bestselling Author, and Podcaster

***

"Drago is a legend in the SEAL Teams as a lead breacher and operator. This book is full of hard-won wisdom and inspiration! He gives a clear image of what it's like to grow up in Communist Poland not long after World War II. His insights will inspire us all to be more grateful for our nation and to be better citizens and better human beings. Given the state of our political environment, we should read Drago's words, listen to his wisdom, and be very careful and diligent to preserve the freedoms that we enjoy. Outstanding read and hard to put down!"
— ED HINER, US Navy SEAL LCDR (Ret),
    Bestselling Author of *First Fast Fearless* and *GUTS*

***

"Drago is the finest Navy SEAL I've had the honor of serving with. Not only was he able to bring together two great units of Special Operations with Polish GROM and US Navy SEALs, but he is most known for his prowess as a Master Breacher. He's the guy who gets the team in and then fights right next to them. Drago's story is one of great appreciation for the freedom he found in America, and his effort to every day give back to America—keeping it the shining beacon of freedom for the world."
— ROB O'NEILL, US Navy SEAL who killed Osama bin Laden,
    Bestselling Author of *The Operator* and *The Way Forward*

***

"As Drago says, we did not go to war to defend freedom for only certain people, we fought for All Americans. His love for this country is infectious, and you will come away from this book with a stronger sense of pride for America and renewed faith in our ability to overcome differences with neighbors to make this country better tomorrow than it is today.

— Marcus Luttrell, US Navy SEAL (Ret), Bestselling
  Author of *Lone Survivor* and *Service: A Navy SEAL at War*

***

"Drago's contribution to our joint, GROM and SEALs, operations has become legendary in Poland among GROM and in the US among his SEAL Brothers, especially his breaching expertise. His new breaching charges allowed us to conduct operations with less risk and less danger to non-combatants on target; while at the same time, with less fragmentation, allowing us to stage in closer proximity to the explosive breach and gain faster access to target."

— Pawel Mateńczuk, Lebanon, Iraq, and Afghanistan Veteran
  of Polish Special Forces GROM

***

"Drago's desire to give back to America for his freedom goes far beyond his incredible service as a Navy SEAL. Drago is also the America-loving patriot, always standing by to remind you of how great this country is and why we need to keep working together as one for the next generation. Drago is a proud, great American, and I am honored to call him my dear friend."

— Rich Emberlin, Dallas Police Dept. SWAT (Ret)

***

"Drago has lived his life taking a stand in the never-ending war for freedom and liberty that each generation must wage against the creeping virus of socialism and totalitarianism. Whether that was on the streets of Poland facing down the Communist and Socialist threat to his homeland or as a decorated US Navy SEAL on the war-torn streets of Iraq, Drago has lived his American value system at the risk of his own life. This book is a must-read for every American who wants to preserve the precious liberty and freedom Lincoln called 'the last best hope on earth.' As an immigrant, his voice rings true for me in a way that I wish every American could understand and stop taking for granted. As citizens of the USA, we owe our country a debt for our freedom. That debt is our loyalty and will to preserve the gift we received for the next generation. My friend Drago has made a major contribution to that effort. Buy this book. Read it. Learn from it. Then act on it."

— SAM FALSAFI, Immigrant from Iran; Lead Trainer, Warrior Week, the world's #1 transformational program for married business men with children

THE PLEDGE
TO AMERICA

ONE MAN'S JOURNEY *from*
POLITICAL PRISONER *to* U.S. NAVY SEAL

DRAGO DZIERAN

Liberatio
Protocol

A LIBERATIO PROTOCOL BOOK
An Imprint of Post Hill Press
ISBN: 978-1-63758-371-5
ISBN (eBook): 978-1-63758-372-2

The Pledge to America:
One Man's Journey from Political Prisoner to U.S. Navy SEAL
© 2023 by Drago Dzieran
All Rights Reserved

Cover Design by Conroy Accord

This is a work of nonfiction. All people, locations, events, and situation are portrayed to the best of the author's memory.

Post Hill Press
New York • Nashville
posthillpress.com

Published in the United States of America
1 2 3 4 5 6 7 8 9 10

*To my fallen Teammates, those lost on the battlefield
and those lost beyond the battlefield.
To America and all of the American people to
whom I owe my freedom and so much more.*

Contents

THIS BOOK IS MY MEMOIR. It reflects my recollections of experiences over time. Some names and other identifying characteristics have been changed, some events have been compressed, and some dialogue has been re-created. What you may currently understand as Communism, Marxism, Leninism, or Socialism may lead you to pause and question how I describe them. Please understand that Eastern European countries under the control of the Soviet Union behind the Iron Curtain are often referred to as Communist. However, none of these states were ever Communist; instead, they were all Socialist states run by Communists and Marxists. This allowed Communists, like my father, to control society and suppress any dissent or opposition, often in a violent way. Regardless of how you choose to accept the labeling, the terror that I and my family endured was real and is described in the following pages in a way that I hope helps you visualize and connect with the true impact of these ideologies upon real people and society.

★ INTRODUCTION ★

IRAQ, 2004

As missions go, this one was standard: approach the compound, breach the doors on the target's house with explosives, and detain the target—in this case, a suspected terrorist. I was confident that it would go off without a hitch, as many of our previous missions in Iraq had.

Working off reconnaissance photos of the compound, as a Lead Breacher, I had prepared the appropriate explosive charges and calculated the safest distance for the rest of the initial assault element to avoid getting caught in the blast. I designated a convenient, safe place that would keep us out of the way of the shock wave and any explosive fragments. It was right behind the corner of the building, between the wall and what looked like a concrete fence. The space was about two to three feet wide and ten to fifteen feet long, enough to safely stack the entire assault element together.

We moved out just after 02:00. We functioned seamlessly as a unit, pushing through the quiet pitch-black night toward the compound rising out of the dusty Iraqi streets. Our orders were to capture or kill the target. We had confirmation that the terrorist was in the building.

The assault element, including myself, scaled the six-foot concrete fence in perfect silence while the designated security element circled the walled compound to make the terrorist's escape impossible (if he decided to run). We hit the ground with barely a rattle. Within moments I was shouldered up against the outer wall of a building just inside the fence, a string of men with me. With practiced movements, I set a breaching charge on the door, and on my signal, my security element and I began to walk back towards the designated space around the corner where the rest of the assault element were already taking cover.

The moment we began to move, however, I realized with a sinking feeling that the reconnaissance images I'd studied earlier hadn't shown the mound of rubble in that same corner between wall and fence.

Shit.

There was barely enough space left to cover most of the assault element. I wasn't going to fit. And there was no time to scale the concrete fence and take cover.

It was a split-second decision: I backed myself as far from the door as possible and then dropped to my knees. I covered my face with my M4, curling up to protect as much of my body as possible. Based on careful calculations for the safe standoff, I knew I would still be relatively "safe" as far as the shock wave was concerned. I learned early on from my previous Direct Action missions to calculate the safe distance from breaching charges in two ways: one normally per the manual, and one for situations like this, for me. The second calculation was important for times when I may not make it to cover but needed to have an absolute minimum safe distance. It was a distance from the breaching charge that could cause injury but should not be incapacitating. I was hoping to never use it. Once I knew everyone had cover, I quietly passed the call over the radio—"Turning steel, turning steel, turning steel!"—and I detonated the charge on the door.

The blast blew the fragments of the door out right over my head with a thunderous sound that rattled my skull. A shock wave that felt like it lifted me off my knees slammed me back onto the ground. I yelled "Open, open, open" even as I tried to regain my footing, only to fall back on my hands and knees, bleeding from my nose and one ear. The breach blew the door wide open, and the rest of the assault element was forced to shove me out of their way as they rushed the building through the smoke. I don't remember pain in the moment. Pain is the last thing on your mind when you're in the middle of an operation.

I rallied quickly enough and joined my team to clear the building, going room to room on autopilot, ears ringing. We caught our suspect without much struggle, and we returned to base on the high of a successful mission before the sun was even up.

Later the next day, when the adrenaline had worn off, I checked myself: some light bleeding from my nose and ears—an expected side effect of taking a shock wave almost directly to the head. The ringing had subsided, but one ear was sore and difficult to hear out of, and I had a massive vivid bruise on the side of my chest that I couldn't account for. I had been wearing steel-plated body armor during the op, but it only covered the front of my chest and my back. It was so sore and ugly looking; I was worried that some fragments from the blast may have bounced off the wall and lodged in the side of my chest. But how could that leave such a massive bruise? Every breaching charge is carefully calibrated, and the one used during the op should not have resulted in any large fragments. Regardless, even a small fragment can maim or kill a person if it penetrates a vital organ or severs a major artery. (Breaching steel doors, steel gates, or concrete walls is especially dangerous in that regard.)

As I inspected the big, ugly bruise on my side, a buddy—one of the Polish GROM guys who was part of the assault element on that mission—came up to me and said, "Sorry, Drago. After the charge went off, you were right in our path, so we had to kind of…kick you out of the way."

Polish GROM (Polish Special Forces) are hardcore operators with impressive combat records. For an average person, a kick like the one I received would have easily broken some ribs or totally incapacitated a person; luckily, I was bulky and had been practicing martial arts for most of my life, so I had some tolerance built in.

My friend smiled, and I laughed. Turns out, *he* was the foot behind my massive mystery bruise. It hurt, but there were no hard feelings; I would have done the same if our situations had been reversed.

☆ ☆ ☆

This is my story.

It's not the story you might expect, coming from a Navy SEAL, but at a time when division and strife are rampant around the world, I think it's an important one to tell. Because just as no two SEALs are the same, neither are any two Americans—and I happen to be both.

I was born in 1960 in Lodz, Poland, deep behind the Iron Curtain. It's important to tell this part of my story in full, and you'll read about it in forthcoming chapters, because my life in Poland directly influenced my coming to America as a political refugee and asylum seeker.

Now I consider myself an American through and through. American by choice. But having been born and raised in Communist Poland, I know what it means to have next to nothing—no money, no safety, no rights—and what it means to come to a place that promises everything. I know how precious those things are and how easily they can be lost, unless someone is willing to step up and fight for them.

This is a story about a life spent fighting, which began well before I picked up a rifle to fight on America's behalf. In houses and classrooms, schoolyards and streets, I learned how to fight, and I learned what to fight for.

I want you to understand that this is not a life I want for anyone—Polish, American, or otherwise. What I want is for no one to have to live like I had to growing up in Communist Poland, a totalitarian oppressive state. I don't want it for anyone anywhere in the world but especially not in America, the country that gave me a home after I lost mine. This memoir is a collection of unforgettable stories from my life: political oppression and persecution, personal desperation, compassion, determination, and—ultimately—sacrifice and courage. This memoir is also my attempt at recalling my life in Poland; it is less about my SEAL experiences from my later years and more about family, faith, and resiliency in the face of adversity. There are plenty of books by and about Navy SEALs, but I wanted to write a book that reflects on what it's like to live under some of the worst circumstances on the planet and to then find freedom in America.

If you came here looking for another typical SEAL memoir, I'm sorry to disappoint you. But I hope you will read this book regardless and maybe come away with a better sense of who you share this beautiful country with and how lucky we all are to live in the greatest country in the world.

Because in the process of learning to be an American, I realized how incredible the American people really are. All of them, regardless of what they look like, how they pray, who they love, or how they vote—this is one country and we are all Americans, and I am honored to fight for them.

CHAPTER ONE

A NEW LIFE

MY LIFE BEGAN IN OCTOBER 1960. Fifteen years after the end of World War II, Poland was still a place of desolation and despair. People were still trying to rebuild their lives after the Second World War, but this time under the terror of the totalitarian state run by Communists and Marxists, like my father. That's where I spent the first years of my life: amid the rusting ruins of the old bombed-out Poland and the cheap scaffolding of the new.

With me were my parents, Stanislaw and Florentyna Dzieran. Following my arrival, my brother, Slawek, and my sister, Justyna, would join us one and four years later, respectively. Together we lived in a standard multi-family home, a two-floor by-the-book Communist build, in a town called Zielona Góra. We lived in the downstairs, which had two rooms for us and a third room for an unrelated single man, a single bathroom, and one rudimentary kitchen we all shared on the first floor. Upstairs there was a duplication of the downstairs floorplan, which another unrelated family occupied. There was no staying out of each other's hair with that many people in one house. Especially when the subject of politics came up.

My father, Stanislaw, was a full-fledged member of the Communist Party in Poland, referred to as the Polish United Workers' Party. He was a well-respected high school teacher until he quit his job to become director of theaters and museums at the Polish Ministry of Art and Culture, working directly for the Polish government. He also worked as the director of the art history department at the University of Lodz. As a proud card-carrying Communist, my father was afforded advantages and luxuries that nonparty members in my country either didn't have or never hoped to get.

Dad was fascinated by technology. Because of his status and connections within the party, he had all kinds of advanced cameras, so I'd often sneak into his closet and play with them. When I got bored, I'd drag his stuff around like a dog at the end of a leash. Eventually he learned to hide things better.

I wish I could say I knew my dad well. At the end of the day, he was a very distant man. Not just to me, but to his entire family. Even from a young age, I only really knew him as a forceful, very logical man who'd show up at the house from time to time between his travels. He would yell at us when we did something wrong, and sometimes he'd hit us with his belt. In his environment, he was very accomplished and respected by the Communist government.

Conversely, my mother, Florentyna, despised Communism, Marxism, and Socialism with a fiery passion. She saw the Communist regime as nothing more than occupiers by a different name, like the Nazis during World War II and the Germans during World War I. She was a devout Catholic, too, which didn't sit well with my father, who believed—per the party line—that it was necessary for Communists to be atheists. He was and remained an atheist until his death in 2021.

My maternal grandmother, similarly, was passionate about church—she would have literally chased my father to church if she could. I remember on one particular Sunday morning when she came to visit, as my parents went through their usual back-and-forth about whether we children would be allowed to go to church that day, my mother grabbed me—Dad was standing in the front doorway, his arms stretched from door frame to door frame as an imposing figure that was not going to let anyone leave—and turned toward the window overlooking the street. To Dad's surprise, she proceeded to hand me straight through the open window to my grandma, who was waiting outside. We went to church. I was too small to remember the lessons from the service on those Sunday church visits, but they were important to my mother.

Dad eventually learned to not interfere with our faith, but he never approved and barely tolerated it. He called it superstition and often ridiculed and disparaged it. And any Sunday that Grandma visited, we went to church. If Grandma wasn't there, we'd go in the evening when Dad was out or wasn't paying attention, but we'd never talk about it at home.

I think I understood even from a young age why both my maternal and paternal grandmothers were so fiercely committed to their faith. My paternal grandmother had witnessed the Communist state's brutal approach to violence during its initial rise. She knew people who were sent to Siberia, to the gulags, even some who were murdered outright for opposing Communism. It must have been devastating for her to watch her own son embrace that ideology and join the party.

My mother's mother, Grandma Maranda, had survived WWI, WWII, and Hitler's Socialism (National Socialism), so she was hardly enthused by Stalin's version and later by Brezhnev's Socialism. The Communist regime used Socialism to subdue society and gain control over the people. These ideologies always have a few of the same things in common: intimidation, political prisoners, political murders, cancellations of people inconvenient to the state, and censorship. My grandmother knew that when times get hard enough, gold and money mean nothing, while faith and belief in God are everything. The only thing that matters in those circumstances is survival: food, water, and shelter. She always saved as much food as possible; during WWII, people would often offer to pay her for a share, attempting to coerce her to sell food that she had saved for her children, but she never accepted it because her family couldn't eat money. She would only give out some bread from time to time to help others who were suffering. Sometimes, while out walking with my grandma, she would find bread on the streets and pick it up while complaining about the waste. Red with embarrassment, I would tell her to put it down while other kids pointed fingers at us and laughed. She'd drop it in a safe place, and then say something like, "Well, at least the birds have something to eat. Never, ever throw food away!"

Despite the tension within the family, we had everything we needed growing up. (What we wanted was irrelevant.) We couldn't afford things like bicycles, so we rode ones that belonged to other kids. As a party member, Dad eventually got a car (which was unusual at the time)—a cheap off-white Syrena, two-doored with a two-stroke engine. That was luxury to us. Normally, people would have to pre-pay the full value of the car and then wait for one to two years to receive the car; however, my dad's position in the party allotted him access to goods much earlier and easier than others.

The thing that sticks out in my mind the most about this time in my life is that we had to walk to kindergarten on our own. At four and five years old, we'd hold each other's hands, carrying our house shoes for school, and walk—half a mile—through a small field outside the apartment complex, across a big street, and all the way to kindergarten. We were essentially on our own; the adults just told us how to get there.

I had my first brush with romance at all of six years old. We were in the same kindergarten class. You know how it goes—one minute we're playing doctors and the next I'm getting kissed on the cheek and have a girlfriend. I think we lasted about a week.

Naturally, kids find all sorts of ways to get into trouble, regardless of the times they live in. Once, playing with gasoline we drained from a parked motorcycle, a bunch of us set fire to it. The thing went up in a fireball and burned my eyebrows right off. On another occasion, while baking potatoes over an open fire, we managed to set fire to a wheat field. By the time the firefighters arrived, the field was completely gone. Some people tried to sue my mom and our neighbors for damages, but there was no money to get out of any of us; besides, my father was able to squash it as a party member. Everything was swept under the table, and people who tried to complain were threatened and easily intimidated by the Socialist state, which my father was part of.

I don't play with fire anymore, and to this day whenever I smell woodsmoke, this exact memory comes back to me.

It's interesting to me now to remember the places where my friends and siblings and I played when we were little kids growing up. A lot of old, dilapidated buildings from before the war were our playgrounds; for poor kids like my brother, sister, and me, the rusting ruins of destroyed textile factories and abandoned prewar buildings were the only spaces for us to play in. Occasionally, new buildings under construction also served as a playground. At that time, everything seemed very large to us. Sometimes I go on Google Maps and look around that old town on street view and see all the places where we used to hang out.

Zielona Góra was granted town privileges in 1323. It has a long and compelling history. When I was growing up there in the 1960s, the city was a small, peaceful town with very little crime. The people's attitudes were different than today. It was okay for me and my siblings to wander around the town, fields, and woods without supervision. My mom let us play outside by ourselves with free rein, as long as we let her know where we were and as long as we were back before dark. When I was five years old, my friend was struck and killed by a motorcyclist. I didn't see it happen, but I saw his body in the open casket at his funeral. It was a horrible sight, and not one I could easily forget. My mom became very strict about my getting to school safely after that. But we were kids, so we'd still mess around and play dumb games like "who can get closest to the moving vehicle."

Later, I would keep it secret from my mom that I'd gotten hit by a motorcycle, too—I was walking out of my first-grade class, feeling like hot shit: I thought I was so important and cool because my mom was a teacher at the school. She was a well-respected teacher in the school, and I felt that nothing could touch me! I started dancing in the street after I noticed some girls watching from the playground and ended up getting clipped by this passing bike. It launched me onto the sidewalk, but I managed to bounce right back up. I was still rattled, though, and immediately ran off across the nearby field, jumped a fence, and sprinted until I was safe at home.

When I did finally tell Mom that story, she gave me a sound spanking.

Father refused to spend much money on our needs, so we couldn't afford to buy the state-required school uniforms, and our grandma—an accomplished seamstress—made them for us instead. The richer kids were quick to point out that our uniforms were not purchased and were homemade. Most of the kids at this time were wearing these homemade uniforms, and I decided to beat the rich kid who opened his mouth first about the uniforms. They left me alone and I never heard about my uniform again. My grandmother had made mine and my siblings' uniforms with her pedaled sewing machine and I would watch the wheel next to her foot go round and round. On one occasion, I happened to notice a pair of sewing shears lying on the floor next to her sewing machine. Stealing it out from under Grandma's nose, I whispered to my little brother, "Let's be barbers."

We hid behind the sofa, and there I grabbed my brother by the hair on the front of his head and *snip, snip, snip!* He did the same to me, snipping away until Grandma, realizing it was far too quiet, jumped up and found us and a pile of hair behind the sofa. We looked like samurai with long hair on the sides but no hair on the top of our heads.

"Oh my god, what did you do?"

She called my mom into the room and told her what had happened. Thankfully, neither of us were physically injured by our antics. Mom sighed heavily and said, "I cannot take you out like this." She shoved hats onto our heads and dragged us to a real barber a few blocks away. Unfortunately, he took one look at my brother and me and said, "I can't do anything with this." There was nothing else to do: he buzzed our heads. Mom cried.

On the dreary walk home, other women berated her for our buzz cuts, telling her, "How could you let these boys walk around looking like criminals?" I hadn't thought of that comparison at the time, but what a thing to hear! (And, as if to add insult to her injury, Mom never stopped giving me grief about the fact that my hair grew back in straight and brown after I'd originally had such beautiful curly blond hair.)

During my primary school years, my mom taught at the same school I was attending, which meant my antics were met with punishment a lot faster too, and with a lot more embarrassment involved. In our underground classrooms, we'd regularly watch for the teacher's arrival through thick half-buried windows, scanning constantly for ankles while we screamed and laughed and teased each other. When one girl made a joke about another girl in class having a crush on me, I puffed up and said, "I don't need a girl!" And then I went up to the girl accused of having a crush on me and kicked her right between the legs. I was violently obstinate. Even as the nurses carried her away crying, I shouted, "She's not my girlfriend!"

I went back to class, and then my mom showed up. It was like the air was suddenly sucked out of the room. She glared right at me, hands on her hips. "Who did you hurt?" The whole class pointed at the girl sobbing at the nearby desk. My mom immediately grabbed me by my ear and neck and pulled me to the front of the room, where she proceeded to spank me in full view of the entire class, so hard and for so long that I broke down and started to cry. After a while, she released me and told me to apologize. The class was silent. I apologized through my tears, and my mom set me back down at my desk before leaving. That day my mother, besides being a very well-respected teacher liked by many students, became a teacher that was feared. None of the kids ever wanted to get on her bad side and test the rules after seeing what happened to me.

When I returned home at the end of school, my mom had an hour-long conversation with me, spanked me some more, and I never hit another girl again.

Corporal punishment was the go-to method in those days, and it was used often, even for minor infractions. If a student ever refused to answer a teacher's question or answered "rudely," the class would go perfectly still, and he would be hit with a wooden ruler on his hand. His ear would be stretched as he was dragged out of the room and spanked, then he'd return to class with tears running down his splotchy face. He'd apologize for not learning and for mouthing off and then very carefully sit back down in his assigned seat. Never mess with teachers in Poland.

Funnily enough, though, the punishment only sometimes managed to deter us from bad behaviors in the long term. It was around this time that my brother and I discovered how fun it was to play hooky. All the bigger kids took over the coolest parts of the playsets and the younger kids were typically pushed to the side, forced to only sit and watch. One morning when we walked by the empty playground on the way to school, we decided to play hooky. So, instead of going to class, we took a detour and went to the kindergarten playground (hidden from prying teachers' eyes behind a bunch of trees) and we'd play our hearts out. We had so much fun, until the angry teachers burst out of the trees and grabbed us both by the waistbands of our cheap pants and all but carried us back to class. Mom would get on the phone and yell at us. We kept doing it, trying not to get caught, but eventually the spankings became more annoying than punishing or funny. At that point, we knew it was time to stop.

My early childhood was full of ups and downs. Life at home was difficult, to say the least, and early learning under Communism was anything but fun. But I can also remember a lot of funny, happy moments, despite all those things. Sometimes it's a big memory like being passed through a window into my grandma's hands or what it felt like to dance in the street for those girls. Other times it's a small memory, like the taste of the special soda we'd buy off Polish street vendors like kids at Coney Island in the summer. It was a mix of fruit juices dyed red and yellow in plain soda water. In a country without access to Coca-Cola, this strange street drink was a real treat to us. Although, in hindsight, I'm amazed that we didn't get sicker off them, considering they were served in reused glasses that didn't get washed very often. One glass was used to serve everyone in the line, with a rinse of the glass only here and there.

It wasn't an easy childhood by any means. And my family would carry a scarcity mentality for life. Because even as other European countries were rebuilding and flourishing in the aftermath of the war, Poland was slowly suffocating to death under the yoke of Socialism behind the Iron Curtain.

CHAPTER TWO

THE STATE OF THINGS

I WAS FOUR, MAYBE FIVE years old the first time I really was made aware of the existence of Communism. At that young age, I didn't understand what it was conceptually, but I recognized its presence in our lives and that it made the adults around me act very strangely.

My own family was a decent representation of Communism's divisive effect. As previously mentioned, my father's mother was an especially vocal anti-Communist. I'd spend time with her and my grandfather when they lived in a little village called Spicimierz. The place didn't even have roads, just dirt paths that got muddy in the rain. My grandparents lived in an old house with a thatched roof. It was drafty and cold, and I didn't like to go there because there was nothing to do except look at farm animals and do chores. In the summertime, the wheat fields had to be cleared and the men would go through them with scythes, cutting the wheat almost at the root. I would follow behind them and tie up small bundles and place them in a pile for collection.

It was hardly a vacation—I wanted to go to stores and ride bicycles and play with toys and eat candy, not *work*.

I remember my grandmother teaching me how to pray during our visits with her. Over and over again I learned the words: how to pray for health, happiness, and liberation. Kneeling next to me, my grandmother would say things like, "Please send the Communists back where they came from" and "Please take the Red Satan away from Poland!" and I would repeat word for word after her.

After repeating her words a few times, I had to ask: "Who are these people?"

"They are evil, they kill people and keep people in prisons. Real demons."

I remember asking my grandmother if they had horns and tails and if they breathed fire. That was my image of Communists. She said yes, but they hide it and many can't see it. We can recognize them most often by their deeds: murders, imprisonments, intimidation, and lack of morals. She fully believed that to be a Communist was a fate worse than death. These were people, she explained to me, who killed other people at will. Why? For not believing everything the party believed in or disagreeing about the benefits of Communism and Socialism. And there wasn't much any innocent person could do about it.

My grandmother's sentiments made for a very strained relationship with her son. My father would get angry when he inevitably learned (or overheard) his mother talking to me about the evils of Communism. He'd demand that she never talk about Communism and Socialism: "Don't talk to my son about that! We're building a Socialist paradise for all of us! I am not evil."

In response, my grandmother would become very still. She would rattle off the names of people she knew who had been imprisoned, disappeared, or murdered—from memory. Dozens of them, years after the fact. My father's pathetic response was always some variation of, "Well, we don't know what really happened."

"Yes," she'd respond, "but if you bring Communism to a place, *that is* what happens."

They'd yell back and forth at each other for hours. My father would shout, and his mother would wave her cane at him.

I'd fall asleep to the sound of her crying. "I should have raised you better."

I loved visits with the other side of my family, with my maternal grandmother in Lodz. Lodz was one of the biggest cities in Poland and always bristling with traffic, tramways, trolleybuses, and cars. It was a fascinating view for me. I remember riding on the escalator in one of the department stores for the first time. It was like a trip to Disneyland for me.

During visits with my maternal grandmother, she would sometimes take my siblings and me to a park outside town with swings and a carousel and a jungle gym. Even though it was a long walk to get there, we were always so excited to go. Twenty minutes on foot was worth it if it meant we got to actually *play*.

The park itself wasn't so much a park as a playground with some trees and trails next to a busy roundabout. The playground area was very flat and unassuming. There was a gravel pit with swings, a seesaw, and plenty of open air. It always smelled nice there, with wildflowers blooming everywhere in the summer. I felt completely unrestricted at the park, far away from parents and chores; there was no one trying to fight me, or vice versa, either. It was usually just me and my brother, and sometimes our friends, playing together.

On one outing, my grandmother fell asleep on a bench while my brother and I played. She was a very short woman, and when she sat down, her feet often dangled over the ground. Her shoes had slipped off her feet a little bit, hanging off her toes. Feeling mischievous, I turned to my little brother and said, "Let's pee in Grandma's shoes."

We thought it was the funniest thing—until she woke up, sprang to her wet feet, and bent us both over her knees for a hard spanking. We walked back to her apartment with her in her wet shoes, leaving wet marks on the pavement. Another thing I never did again.

I have a lot of happy memories of my maternal grandmother, which I'm grateful for. I remember she would buy fresh strawberries and mash them with sugar for our breakfast. I'm pretty sure that's what got me hooked on sugar; even tomatoes, sliced and sprinkled with sugar, tasted just like strawberries (a trick my father had learned during the war). When the whole family got together to have dinner, my brother and I would steal shots of vodka and hang out on her balcony. We discovered we could stick our heads and bodies through the bars of her sixth-floor apartment and crawl out onto the side of the building and hang out there for minutes at a time. We got up to thirty minutes once, until a neighbor spotted us and immediately told our parents. Grandma wasted no time hauling us back inside to give us another spanking.

☆ ☆ ☆

The state infiltrated every aspect of our lives. Learning the Russian language, for example, became mandatory when I entered the fifth grade. Even at that young age I was precocious: I openly questioned why we had to learn Russian when there were people who didn't even know Polish fully—after all, the Russians were occupiers. That didn't go over well in my school. My mother was no longer teaching in the same school as me and was unable to provide the usual first line of punishment. So, my teacher immediately pulled me out of class and marched me straight to the principal's office. Once I was standing in front of him, he called the police. On their way to the school, the police grabbed my mom out of her school across town and sat us all down for a talk. In addition to the uniformed police officers, a member of the state security police, in plain clothes (likely a member of the SB—Służba Bezpieczeństwa), joined the police during the questioning of my mother.

"If this happens again—if we hear anti-Communist and anti-Polish sentiments expressed again," they said, "he's going to an orphanage, and you'll be facing prison time for failing to teach your children the right way to think."

The regime felt they knew best how to raise the children of Poland and would not hesitate to remove children from homes of anyone deemed a threat to the Communist Party.

The reality is that anything spoken not in favor of Socialism and Communism was immediately translated by the Communist government as anti-Polish sentiment. I still remember those words and my mom's cries as she promised to work with me on how I expressed myself. I'd behave next time.

Very sternly they replied, "There won't be a warning next time."

At that time, everything that was or seemed like an anti-Communist sentiment was immediately branded as anti-Polish, too, and criminal in nature. The totalitarian government criminalized everything that was not along the Communist Party lines.

That was the first taste I personally got of Communist control. Up to that point, I thought the regime was something my parents had to deal with; I was just a kid! What harm could I do? Enough to bring the state security police down on my head, apparently.

When my father abandoned us to take a job with the Communist-run government in Zielona Góra in 1967, I was seven years old and had been around the man often enough to know he wasn't really interested in sticking around. I think he was tired of having a big family, or he simply wanted to start over with a new one. Or perhaps, it was more the Christian faith of my mother and our family that drove him away so he could find success within the Communist Party.

Mom, meanwhile, was left to care for us on her paltry teacher's salary. I still remember her leaving the house before dawn to stand in line at five o'clock in the morning, every morning, waiting her turn to buy a loaf of bread. On many days, the bread was gone before she reached the front of the line. The food shortages meant my siblings and I often went to school hungry. There usually wasn't much to eat when we got home either. Bread, butter (when we had it), and a cup of tea was a staple. Mom often was able to get a chicken or something to cook for us, and we never complained. We didn't think that it could be any better.

Despite our struggles, I knew my mother was doing the best she could. During Poland's frigid winter months, she stuffed my regular clothes with crumpled-up newspapers to keep me insulated from the cold. She kept a stiff upper lip, my mother, and tried not to let on how difficult things were. On one particularly frigid, blustery day while walking home together as a family, I remember seeing her shiver violently. I realized how cold she was and immediately began removing the crushed newspapers from my coat to give to her. She was petrified that someone could be watching and see that we did not have warm clothes and only stuffed papers in our clothes. It was embarrassing to her. She wept in the street that day, wishing out loud that she could do more for us.

Things went from bad to worse after my father left home. In Poland, there was a stigma for families who were divorced. Children of divorced parents were called names, and many times other families would not allow their children to play with the children of a divorcée. I was in the first grade, and we were forced to look for a different house with little warning. This wasn't an easy process either—like most things in Communist countries, everything operated with at least some degree of difficulty, especially for a single mother of three.

Eventually the car went away with my father, too, along with what little money my mother made and her general control of our lives. The house we lived in was tiny, as I mentioned earlier, and shared with whomever the Communist government assigned to live there. Since I grew up with strangers always around at home, I saw nothing wrong or strange with the arrangement. My mother, however, always found ways to complain about living with strangers and wanted to find a better place for our family. She couldn't choose a different house or apartment after my father left (houses and apartments were assigned to you by the state) and had to accept whatever she was given. She petitioned the government for a different location, and after a year we were finally allocated a new place to live. We moved to a little apartment across town, almost six miles from where we had been living before. At that age, in that place, that was a huge distance, especially since we had to walk or take the bus everywhere.

Despite our circumstances, my mother did her best by her three kids. She'd buy me a monthly allotment of bus tickets for getting to and from school. I still had to walk a half mile to the bus stop, take the bus for a handful of miles, and then walk another half mile to school. But I felt independent and cool being on my own. Back home, my mother and sister occupied one of our two rooms; my brother and I had the other. Our beds were narrow and the mattresses were thin, much like the walls. To be able to sleep on cold nights, we shoved our beds together and slept head to feet to fit side by side.

To say Polish winters are very cold would be putting it mildly. It was bad enough that we had to stuff our coats with old newspaper to keep warm; the fact that we couldn't afford to replace them with coats that could actually keep us warm was worse. It turned out that my father was refusing to pay child support, so while we were trying to hide our crinkling coats from other kids, he was buying a new life for himself. The court eventually forced him to start paying, which he did, but always late.

This was too much for my mother. She told my sister to go to see our father and ask him to increase child support so she could buy warm coats for all of us. Justyna did as she was told, traveling to our father's home with our mother. Father refused, telling his young daughter, "I won't give a penny more than what the court decides. It is up to your mother to buy you warm clothes."

Even living two miles away, that man went to a lot of effort to avoid us. Sometimes we would make a surprise visit, hoping that maybe he would be excited to see us. Approaching his new place, we could see the lights on, but he'd never come to the door when we knocked. So eventually I said, "Screw it," and started pulling pranks and messing with his property, using whatever I could get my hands on to leave a mark.

On top of all this, we were often hungry. That loaf of bread my mother got if she was early and lucky enough? You couldn't buy more than one loaf at that time; people could get violent if you tried. I once asked my mother what would happen if someone tried to steal more than their share. "You'd be lynched," she replied.

This meant we were forced to learn ways to be less hungry. Soon, my brother learned how to make french fries from potatoes while I learned to spot the school children of wealthy Communist Party members by their sandwiches.

These were some good-looking sandwiches, too. While my siblings and I were eating thin sandwiches with butter (or margarine if there was no butter), often only sprinkled with sugar, these rich kids were eating theirs with fresh meat and all the best fixings, dressing smeared across their smug faces.

There were two ways to get your hands on nice things in those circumstances: money and violence. And since we were poor, I used violence. This is where I learned that violence works; if violence didn't work for you, it meant you didn't apply enough of it.

I'll be the first to admit that I was a bully as a kid. Sometimes it was justified, and sometimes it was just what had to be done. Living in blocks (what Americans might call projects), gangs of older kids would pick fights from apartment to apartment and then eventually move on to building to building and street to street. They were always escalating things. They liked to single me out and jump me on my way home from school.

Since I hadn't quite gotten the hang of using my hands in self-defense (I was only nine years old at this point), I decided to start carrying a steel pipe in my school bag. If someone followed me, I'd hide in a stairwell or behind a door and meet him, pipe in hand. I only had to use this a few times because after the word spread about mean kids not leaving the stairways after following me, they left me alone. Again, violence always worked for me. If it didn't work, it meant I didn't apply enough of it, and I was getting better at applying it every day.

This happened a few times. One kid immediately backed down and promised to bring me fresh fruit and other fancy things as long as I didn't hurt him. An older boy, a big seventeen-year-old who lived in our building, made the mistake of hitting me and my little brother. We hit him back. My brother and I were wearing skates and we kicked him until he ran away crying.

That night, we got a knock on the door. A mom and dad stood there in the hallway with their son, whose face was swollen and who seemed a bit weak in the knees. He was much older and about a foot taller than me and my brother.

"Your son almost killed my son!" the woman screeched. "He may never have children—look at what they did to him! Show them what they did to you!" The boy unzipped his pants right then and there. He stood naked in our doorway, his bruised anatomy exposed for anyone to see.

My mother looked down at me. "Did you do this?"

"Yes," I admitted, "because he hit Slawek and he tried to hit me!"

She looked at the crying boy and made a face like she'd sucked on a lemon. "They had every right to defend themselves—look how big he is. He started the fight; they taught him a lesson."

The lesson I learned was that violence solved problems for me. I had only one other time where a parent came to my mom to complain about her son being beat up. It was later when I already had taken up boxing and hit another kid for beating my little brother at school. His nickname was Bull. He was two grades older than my brother and a head taller. When my brother came back from school, we thought that he had been hit by a car. His face was swollen and his head was square like a dice. I was sick at that time, running a fever, with a doctor's excuse from school and orders to stay in bed. After hearing what happened, I was ready to go back to school. My mother knew what I was going to do, and she firmly forbid me to leave the house. I had to wait until the next morning, after she left to work. I went straight to school and waited for a break between classes. As I walked up to him, I realized how much bigger than me he was. He recognized me and tried to put up a fight. Two punches—one to the gut, one in the nose—and the kid, known as Bull for being the school bully, flew down an entire flight of stairs, landing unconscious with a thud. As I was leaving, I remember seeing him being carried by students and teachers to the nurse's room. I went back home and stayed in bed for the rest of the day, as the doctor required, until my mom returned home from work. I never told her, and thought this was the end of the story. However, in the evening the doorbell rang. It was Bull with his mom demanding a strong punishment for the fight. Bull had both eyes swollen, one of them we could not even see, and he was crying profusely. I was thinking, *Good shot.* The woman screamed at us that her son may lose his eye, but then my little brother was called in. He looked almost as bad as this "Bull" guy. My mother mused how such a big guy got so beaten up by a much smaller guy like me. But in the end, she told them that next time her bully son would lose his teeth along with his eye, and she threw them out of our apartment. When I returned to school after being sick, I could see this "Bull" kid during breaks between classes, standing quietly in the hallway with a big white patch on his left eye. He never bothered anybody again. Once again, my method worked!

I remember watching with envy the Communist Party kids with their fancy sandwiches at school; I knew I had to do something and I would. I walked right up to one of them and grabbed the food right out of their hands. The first time I did it, I took a huge bite and said, stunned, "Holy shit! This is an awesome sandwich. I really like it! Where did you get this?"

"My mom and dad made it," the nervous kid replied.

I chewed thoughtfully for a minute. Then I told him, "Here's what's going to happen: Your mom is going to make two sandwiches, and you're going to bring both to school tomorrow. Just tell your parents that you are growing and feel like eating more." (My mom was always telling me that I was growing and needed to eat more.) "Tomorrow, if you don't give me one, I am going to eat your sandwich."

I wasn't much bigger than this boy, but he was soft and well fed. My intimidation attempt was a success. He brought two sandwiches to school the next day and gave me one, as we'd discussed.

This arrangement quickly reached a point that I could confidently tell my mom not to worry—I was not hungry and I couldn't eat lunch even if I wanted to. I told her this so she didn't have to worry about stretching the one paltry loaf she got every morning. She never said so, but I think she was relieved by this. She never found out, or I would have been spanked, marched through the school, and forced to apologize to the kids that I was extorting for sandwiches.

I noticed that there were a couple other kids like me who didn't eat as much as they should and whose mothers were struggling like mine was. You could spot them easily as they were the ones not eating meals during the breaks, or they would hide their meager sandwiches and eat when nobody could see. They also didn't want to tell people they were poor. When your pride is one of the few things you do own, it can be hard to let go of. I'd tell these kids that I was eating like a king, pilfering delicious sandwiches off rich Communist Party kids who'd never been kept up a single night with gnawing hunger. I promised them I'd get more sandwiches, or at least teach the other poor kids what to say so they'd get fed, too. We had almost every rich party kid in my class bringing two sandwiches every day and sharing them with the kids who didn't have one. I remember only one time when one of them complained and their parent came to school enraged. Well, before this kid had a chance to identify me as the culprit during class, I used my persuasion technique during the break. I took this kid and busted his lips, and he agreed he didn't recognize anybody in our class who was stealing his sandwiches. We all came to the conclusion that it had to be some kid from a different, older class. His parents made sure that this big kid, Artur, only brought one sandwich to school. They never found out that every day, he was only eating half of his sandwich. He never complained again. We all got our sandwiches in the end.

Other things were incredibly precious to us poor kids. Bubble gum was the most expensive commodity, and the hardest to find. It basically functioned as currency for us kids. What we'd do was chew the gum, rewrap it, and sell it back to the rich party kids for five Polish złoty, making enough money to pay for the sandwiches outright. We could have paid, anyways; we didn't, though. Swindling rich kids out of money for candy was way more fun.

This was my way of earning a living (and putting food in hungry bellies) for a few years. By the time I was entering eighth grade, my mom couldn't afford to support me, by then almost thirteen years old, plus two other young children. So, she did the only thing she could do and sent me to live with my father.

This wasn't an easy decision for her to make, or for my father to accept. He was already remarried at this point, and had recently moved to Warsaw where he was living happily with his new wife and her young son. Since it was a seven-hour train ride for us from Zielona Góra, he no longer had to worry about unannounced visits. However, my father did not tell his wife that I was coming to visit, let alone coming to live with them. I still remember the eyes of his wife when she opened their door and stared at me, screeched, and wailed, "What!" like she was horrified.

I didn't see any point in telling her that this arrangement was no pleasure for me either. I missed my mother, even my annoying younger siblings. My father's wife resented my being there and did everything to make my stay as miserable as possible, picking on me and making me do menial chores for hours on end, so I decided to make her son's life miserable as well, to the point that he would hide in his room for hours to avoid me. There was no using violence in my father's house, but I was an angry teenage boy—I didn't have to be too violent to be insufferable.

Every conversation with my father went to politics because my views of Communism and Socialism were not to his liking. They were based on my mother's views and my experiences as a young teenager. During arguments with my father, he tried to convince me that "superstitions" of church and God were out of date and must therefore be abandoned and changed. The Communist Party was working on that change, teaching people how to see the world with new values. He believed that we needed to support the Communists with the new worldview and those who did not support it would eventually be eliminated as they would be a danger to the new society. He was very adamant about it; however, he was never able to convince me of his Socialist relative morality.

Before moving in with my father and his new family, I started boxing training in a police club in Zielona Góra. Turns out, I was a natural at it. Plus, I got to practice regularly outside the gym and develop some of my other more nefarious skills. In fact, these skills proved quite useful when finding my way around Warsaw.

You see, even though we lived in Communist Poland, in a world of restrictions, contraband, and rigid rules, there was plenty of illegal stuff happening. You just had to know where to look and how to fight.

There were groups of kids in schools across the city who would extort alcohol from party members' kids and then sneak it onto school grounds to share with their friends. One day, after beating up a guy I'd caught being mean to some girls I knew, a group approached me at school. They were my kind of people: extortionists who wanted to take from the rich to give to the poor and who didn't care how it happened. They told me to go rough up some party kids for booze; in response, I beat up two of them and a third ran off. I understood their motivations, but I wasn't at their beck and call either. Once they understood that I was their equal, I told the two remaining hustlers, "I won't beat you up, *and* I'll bring you what you want."

And I kept my word. Using the money I got from the gum venture, I'd buy a big bottle of wine and give it to the hustlers. I didn't dare drink any of it. I knew my dad would kill me if he smelled alcohol on me. And I'd had enough of his beatings for a lifetime.

I only lived in Warsaw for one year.

The end of that school year marked the end of my elementary school experience. To celebrate the occasion, the school would throw a graduation party, but you had to pay the required amount to attend. The collection happened at the same time my father was out of town on business, leaving his wife in charge. I asked her to pay the fee so I could go to my own graduation, but she refused.

I was crushed. Rather than wait for my father to come home so I could plead my case, I jumped on the first train back to Zielona Góra. A letter from my father to my mother was not far behind: in it, he told her I was not allowed to return to live with him, which was fine by me. I didn't miss him, and I didn't miss his new family either.

But life in Zielona Góra hadn't gotten any easier in the year I'd been away.

CHAPTER THREE

KEEPING FAITH

COMMUNIST POLAND WAS THE SECOND most populated country within the Eastern Bloc. With so many people to suppress, Communist Party officials worked hard to stifle freedom as much as they could, in as many places as they could. They had to if they wanted to maintain control and ensure they were "elected" again.

Living under Communism meant a lot of necessities and other aspects of our day-to-day lives were restricted, if not withheld outright from us. Even years after the end of the war, Poland was still a shadow of its former self, struggling to recover. Many of its people—at least anyone who wasn't a party member—were looking over their shoulder.

The reality was, if you said one wrong thing in front of the wrong person, you risked being questioned about your loyalty to the Communist state, interrogation, imprisonment, and all kinds of awful punishments. Many people lost their jobs, friends, and family, seemingly out of nowhere. If the regime deemed someone a threat, the regime would spread rumors behind their backs to anyone that would listen. These were very deliberate tactics of the Communist state where they would quietly discredit the individuals, making false accusations and claims of any crime they could think of (rape, pedophilia, theft...). Artists were pushed out of the mainstream, writers were no longer published, painters were no longer able to showcase their work, and people could not even get an interview for jobs they had decades of experience with. This cancellation of people was done by state security police in addition to the very public intimidation and censorship by the government. Innocent people did not know why these things were happening to them. Others lived in fear of being targeted next, and some would even shun the targeted person if they thought doing so would keep themselves safe. You never knew who the informant was that was snitching to the state security police.

Growing up, I didn't get sent off to school with a little packed lunch and a kiss on the cheek. My mother was terrified of retaliation, and she warned us almost every morning before we went to school to not speak about politics, Communism, Socialism, or the party. "Don't repeat anything you hear the grandmothers say. Eventually the time will come that we will be able to speak freely," she'd tell us.

For years I didn't understand why, but when it came to my mother, I did as I was told and didn't say anything to anyone.

Living under a constant state of oppression, people were desperate to speak their minds. Very often, they would go to church just to have the chance. Within the relative safety of the church, the priests would speak against the state's oppression in sermons, and people ate it up. Doing this wasn't without risk: some of those priests who delivered such sermons were shot, but not all of them. Often the state-run media would publicly denigrate the priests and churches, making a mockery of faith in an attempt to turn people away from the church. These priests were heroes to us either way. Just one or two words from a priest made all the difference; they gave us hope. They told us to look to the history of Poland and places like America for guidance and courage.

"Look how free Poland used to be, how free other countries and their people are. Hope for that."

As we listened to these sermons and tried to cling to that faint sense of hope, Poles were outside fighting each other for bread. But we needed something to hold on to besides our rage, our hunger, and our hatred of the Communists. The hope for democracy became that thing.

In the meantime, the church was our shelter. It was one of the only places where we felt free to speak and think differently. Despite the regime's best efforts to destroy our sense of faith and deter us from going, we went. People who didn't even believe in God went to church just for a chance to speak their minds or listen to others speak theirs. The state security police were omnipresent, in the church and around the church. The oppression was that intense. People literally risked their lives and jobs to go to church.

The church didn't mean nearly as much to us kids as it did to older people like my mother, her mother, and others who had lived through the war. I was too young to appreciate its importance in our lives. But as I grew up, I would go with my family to show my support (if I wasn't forced to after being passed through a window like a football). For me, when I was only about four years old, church mostly consisted of me jumping on people's bent backs when they got on their knees to pray. I loved to run as fast as I could and dive onto them, complete strangers who were often my grandmother's age. It was quite a laugh when we'd tumble to the church floor together—at least, it was to me. In hindsight, I'm amazed they never tried to stop me.

As I got older, though, I wanted to be more independent and didn't want to spend my time in church, listening to a weird language I didn't understand, when I could be outside playing with the other kids. I soon realized if I offered to go to church by myself, I could make up a sermon and report back to my mother and grandmother and instead spend that valuable time in the boxing ring or on the playground. Eventually they caught on and secretly followed me to church to make sure I actually went. Grandma spanked me for that. When my siblings tried to do it with me, they got spanked, too, and then we gave it up.

We simply weren't old enough to appreciate the fact that the Catholic Church played a huge role in Poland surviving Communism and Socialism, whether it was Stalin-Socialism, Hitler-National Socialism, or Khrushchev-Socialism. All of these ideologies were violent, intimidating and murdering political dissidents. However, faith and the church provided the hope needed to survive. Whereas it was a tedious chore to us kids, it was a safe haven for our parents and grandparents. These were people who had watched the Nazis sweep through years before and wipe whole villages and cities off the map. That they still had a church to worship in was nothing short of a miracle to many people, even if doing so put their lives at risk. The Communists put a great deal of effort into destroying faith, family, and morality. The independent thinking of Polish people was viewed as dangerous to the totalitarian government. Church helped to keep focus on family values and morality, and provided the strength to not be swayed by political ideology. Faith was a form of resistance, and in resistance, people found hope.

My education in Communist oppression never let up for a moment. In 1973, before I went off to live with my father for that one miserable year, a classmate of mine experienced its cruelty firsthand. We were in the same class, but he was a wealthy, popular Communist Party kid, so we weren't all that friendly or close. But I knew him well enough to notice when he stopped showing up to class. That lasted until school let out for vacation. I eventually sought him out; he invited me over to his family's apartment, where he told me his mother had recently died.

This was absurd to me. Surely there was medicine she could have been given.

"The doctors told her she was too old to bother saving," he told me. "That they were saving the medicine for younger people."

The reality, I learned, was that regardless of whether medications or cancer treatment would have saved his mother, there simply wasn't enough supply in Poland to treat everyone in need. That doctors were rationing lifesaving medications for younger people was sad and shocking.

I told my mom about what happened when I got home that evening. Her face was sad but resigned as she replied, "That's very common." It was a tactic frequently used by the Communists as a way to force people to comply. Often, people were made to understand that the best medicine was only available to "good citizens," those who supported the Communist Party.

She went on to explain the concept of "relative morality" to me. She talked at length about Stalin and Hitler's versions of Socialism and how people can be swayed to not think for themselves when they subscribe to ideologies that don't hold solid moral values but instead are purely the values of individual politicians or the leading political party. After all, she explained, Jewish people were technically considered equal to Germans until the politics changed; when politicians started changing the nation's values, Jewish people were cast as villains, and the Holocaust ensued.

"It starts with 'don't buy from Jewish people,' and then it becomes 'destroy their businesses,' and then it's 'imprison them,' and then finally it's 'exterminate them,'" she said. What was once unthinkable became real and acceptable because individual politicians convinced enough people to adjust their values to match those in power. And by that point, it was too late. My mother called it *relative morality*— morality that was not anchored in faith and solid foundations, but was based on the whim of a politician or political party.

My father, a devout Communist, was at the forefront of this in Poland's attempt at Socialism. Back when we all lived together, he'd say things like, "Don't be a Jew," an anti-Semitic way of telling someone, "Don't be a thief." My mother would cry whenever she heard him say it. They would have massive arguments that ring in my ears to this day: "You are dehumanizing an *entire segment of society*. You are worse than animals! Your mother is right—you *are* the devil." But my father was always adamant that he and the rest of the Communists were right. He believed that he was at the forefront of building a better world for humanity, and that it required some sacrifice, including eliminating people opposing the Socialist paradise.

I didn't hate anyone, but I heard friends and classmates say all kinds of things in school, like, "Give me a dollar for a drink, don't be a Jew." It was so commonplace; I didn't really think twice about it. I wouldn't say it, because I knew my mom would spank me if she heard me, and I already understood it was wrong, but it was everywhere. We weren't allowed to say anything bad about anyone at home. We could argue with each other's views, but we couldn't dehumanize them. That's the great irony: even the worst people are still people at the end of the day.

And even though I was too young to understand the politics behind a lot of things, I was able to hear things like anti-Semitic slang and connect it to Poland's Communist system. Homeless people "didn't want to work," so they were ostracized and neglected. When the government executed citizens, they were called "bandits" and "insurrectionists" and "enemies of the state," people who were trying to upend the "successful" Socialist system. Societal values had changed, and the thinking became that these people should be isolated from society, in some cases executed, for opposing Socialism and the official Communist Party line. Show trials were publicly prosecuted. A lot of charges against said "insurrectionists" were completely made up; evidence was made up and there was no opportunity to challenge the charges. People were harassed by state security police and publicly humiliated; they were isolated from friends and businesses. The Communist regime was relentless in pursuit of dissidents. They did not need to have any evidence; they would manufacture the evidence. There were countless victims.

To this day, no one knows how many, and Poles continue to find secret graves of the opponents of Socialism and Communism in prison courtyards, forests, and other obscure places. To this day, Poles are searching for the graves of their World War II heroes who disappeared or were outright murdered by Communists upon their return from the war.

CHAPTER FOUR

THE FIGHT

AFTER MY FATHER KICKED ME out and back to Mom, I thought I would be done with upheavals for a while. The back and forth had been upsetting and stressful, and I was excited to go back to my friends and classmates in Zielona Góra in 1975. But I was also drinking and smoking and had decided to take up karate after getting a taste of boxing in Zielona Góra and Warsaw. I was a lot of trouble for my mom, to say the least.

I first got involved in *kyokushin*, a form of karate, that same year. I was not quite eighteen yet, and I knew my mother wasn't about to give her permission, so I took my school ID and scraped my birth date off very carefully and changed my birth year from 1960 to 1957. Of course, the age restriction wasn't the only barrier I had to overcome if I wanted to learn karate; the next issue became how to pay for classes. My mother's financial woes hadn't changed in the year I'd lived with my father; it was still a daily struggle for her to make ends meet. But she told me that if I worked hard collecting and recycling glass bottles for money, she would pitch in for my tuition. I didn't stop at recycling; I was so determined to take the class, I started stealing whole bundles of newspapers late at night just after they were dropped off to be sold, hiding them in our basement until dawn, and then selling them the next day as recycling paper.

But it wasn't long before upheaval reared its ugly head again. My mother, who was about at her wit's end with three kids back in the house (including two teenage boys), decided it was time to leave Zielona Góra and return to Lodz. She was so desperate for community and family and friends, even if it meant trading our apartment for a studio. This was extremely stressful in Communist-controlled Poland. We had to wait on the government to approve the move and had to accept whatever they gave us or find someone willing to trade homes with us. The trade is what happened the soonest, and the other family happily took our two-room apartment in exchange for their studio in Lodz. We moved, and we lived there for two years until Mom could secure a two-bedroom apartment. But until then, it became so unbearable that my brother offered to go stay with our father despite my mother's wishes to stay together as a family. She eventually relented and allowed him to go. In my mother's mind, it was a terrible tragedy to give up one of her children, but the load on the family was just too much. He and I joked that it was his turn to go. My brother had a lot of friends and got along better with people. He played violin, my sister played piano, and I beat people up. Maybe that's why he and our father got along so well and why my brother was able to stay there until he graduated from high school, whereas I'd only lasted a year.

Now back in Lodz, my birthplace, I was determined to stop letting these upheavals affect me. Karate kept me focused and disciplined. I soon switched to taekwondo, where I learned that the people there trained on the street as much as they did in the dojo.

Our instructor was from Laos, and he was very open about the importance of learning things in class while simultaneously stressing the need to practice techniques on the street. I had plenty of adolescent street-fighting skills, and combined with my nascent martial arts training, I felt well equipped to do what the man said. So we'd walk around and pick guys on the street—vagrants, drunks, bullies, gangsters—to fight.

At that time and in that place, street fighting was very common. It was barely frowned upon. In fact, it was common to see people fighting in the streets in the city. Passersby quickly learned to just cross the street whenever they encountered a brawl.

I never worried about having the police called on us or about anyone else interfering. The fights themselves were relatively self-contained, with few—if any—bystanders getting caught in the crossfire. We eventually started to run out of people to train on. Old bums and drunks were no longer fun or even a challenge. As we improved our skills, we were seeking out people who looked more like they could handle a fight and offer somewhat of a challenge. Sometimes we would draw lots on who would fight a particular group of people, and would sometimes intervene if the group turned out to be too much for one of us to handle individually. After these fights, we would share observations and critiques with each other on techniques used and effectiveness to keep improving our skills.

Since sparring in the gym could only teach us so much, street fighting became my second classroom. I didn't just want to be good at fighting, I wanted to be effective so I could handle whatever situation I found myself in. For two to three hours every day I'd work out, run, and practice at the gym; if we didn't practice there, we'd go out on the street and pick targets. Eventually we started doing the fighting part on our own. We'd have some drinks after class and then individually roam the streets, beating people up.

Like a lot of things involving adrenaline, eventually we started chasing bigger fights. My friends and I would harass groups of two, three, four people—usually those who'd been drinking and looked tough. Sometimes we'd get tangled up with police, especially if we were beating up multiple people, which takes longer. But in those instances, we'd just cut and run, confident that the police wouldn't bother chasing after kids for petty infractions, which most of the time they didn't.

Learning how to fight was a discipline and a form of exercise that required focus, commitment, and humility. Fighting, on the other hand, was an outlet. Being a teenager is hard enough, even at the best of times; being a teenager in Communist Poland in the '70s was downright brutal. I still have the scars to show for it.

★ CHAPTER FIVE ★

UNDER OUR THUMB

AS I GREW OLDER, MY understanding of what it meant to live in a Communist state grew with me. It's easy to be young and naive, but for me and a lot of other kids who grew up hungry in borderline poverty, naivety was a privilege we didn't have.

If a student didn't show up at school, the police, at the request of a teacher, were allowed to find them, pick them up, and call their parents down to the station. On the streets of Poland, police patrols would often stop young people who were of school age to check their IDs. "Documents please," is how they would approach the students. They would check for the student ID and ask why they were on the streets and not in school.

You had better have a valid excuse or you could be detained and then hauled back to school. If a student was sick, they had to have a certified note from a doctor prescribing bed rest for three to four days. (Kids would do all kinds of weird stuff to try and get "sick." Some said eating raw potatoes would give you a fever, but it just made my stomach ache.) It couldn't be as simple as copying a signature either; doctors had their own identifying rubber stamps so people couldn't forge prescriptions. I would write my own requests for bed rest and, using a fine-point red fountain pen, draw a doctor's stamp with a name, address, number, everything. My artistic skills were so keen that I was able to precisely replicate the stamp so it was indistinguishable from the real stamp, and no one ever caught me.

I love drawing. I often drew entire comic books in the class to make other kids laugh. One of my professors' names was Rycerz (which means "Knight" in English). I had a field day with him every time he showed up in class, until one day he got hold of one of the drawings I did about him, titled: Przygody Rycerza Zakutej Paly (loosely translated to "adventures of the knight who is a thick-headed idiot"). He didn't like it very much. I got myself in trouble once again.

The older I got, the more I took "fighting oppression" literally. I was always ready to brawl with someone, or at least give them a bad headache with my behavior. Like most teenagers, I was rebellious, and the fact that I lived under an oppressive Communist regime gave me that many more opportunities to cause trouble.

But my rebelliousness wasn't new. I was noticing the police were not just stopping the school kids out of classes to check documents; they were stopping anyone. It was common for them to randomly stop people on the street to check documents. They were looking for your personal ID book, known as "dowód osobisty." These documents were actually entire booklets filled with a variety of your personal information such as: your name, address, both parents' names, social hierarchy classification (inteligencia, physical worker, etc.), your workplace, and a rubber stamp from the workplace with the signature from an official at your workplace. This booklet contained every address you had ever lived and every workplace you had ever worked. If you did not have your booklet on you or if the police reviewed your documents and found there were inconsistencies or an invalid stamp, you were likely to be detained until it was cleared up. This often meant a drive to the police station until the documents were straightened out. This was the reality of life, and for a long time I didn't think it was odd or should be different because it was all I knew. That was just the way things were.

I started listening to Voice of America, the BBC, and Radio Free Europe years before. Without anyone knowing, I began tuning in shortly after my run-in with the state security police, after I'd questioned my teacher about being forced to learn Russian.

I had been told about these radio channels by my mother's brother. Uncle Adam despised Communism and was actively resisting Communist indoctrination in Poland. He was an inspiration to me: As a younger man, he had opened a storefront for manufacturing bricks and concrete blocks. His product was so good and his business so reliable that construction companies stopped ordering from the government factories and instead bought from him directly. This, of course, angered the government, and they brought the police down on him. He was told to either scale down his business to the point that it was no longer competitive or shut down entirely. He said he couldn't afford to do either; at an impasse, a group of young men claiming to be anti-fascist demolished my uncle's machines and beat him, and the police dragged him to prison, where they beat him some more.

He wasn't there long. Despite the whole family's protests, my uncle was determined to keep at his one-man resistance movement. He taught people how to make cement, and he showed me how to listen to banned radio stations. Unfortunately, this kept him on the police's radar. He was beaten and imprisoned several times; it was an intimidation tactic more than anything else, something they did to a lot of people, often on trumped-up charges. My uncle was marked as an opponent of Socialism and was regularly harassed and beat up by thugs at the direction of the state security police and the local Communist Party. One of our more outspoken neighbors was disappeared in this way, but unlike my uncle, he never came back. His wife tried to ask after him, but the police's response was clear: if she kept asking questions, she would be gone too.

But one thing can be said about Poles—they always find ways of fighting back. While there were plenty of Communist sympathizers, followers, and politicians, the general population hated Communism and tried their best to resist it in whatever ways they could. My uncle became a local mascot for what happened to anti-Communists, but he wore the title proudly. After every beating he received, he would return home black and blue, but even more determined. His captors told him: "Tell your neighbors—this is what happens when they step out of line."

I thought he was incredibly brave. Listening to the radio was a risk, but I wanted to be like my uncle. My mother was always panicking about it—she had to explain to me that regardless of whether they sent me to prison, she *definitely* would lose her job if the authorities had solid evidence that

I was listening to illegal channels. Suppressing unauthorized frequencies was a necessary business in Communist Poland. The regime-built radio transmitter towers were designed specifically to overpower the radio frequencies of Voice of America and Radio Free Europe. These towers were built all over Eastern Europe. But like a lot of Soviet-era tools and devices, they didn't work as well as they were supposed to. I'd turn on those channels and at first only hear a deep *woom, woom, woom*, but if I turned it up loudly enough, I could hear voices. Broadcasters. The first time I was able to catch a few minutes of a Voice of America broadcast, I learned about Poland's ongoing disinformation campaigns. My mother caught me, and although she understood, she demanded I do something to make it quieter so the neighbors would not hear, so I buried my head and the radio under blankets and pillows and listened to the broadcasts that way.

I kept at it for years. I listened to contraband radio as often as I could, well into my late teens. Getting information about my country from outside my country was mind blowing. I had been so accustomed—almost indoctrinated—to the Communist Party line for so long that the actual unbiased truth was shocking. The Soviet Union and other Communist states were intensely committed to lying about anything that reflected poorly on Socialism and Communism. Historical figures were erased from history; monuments not along party lines were toppled, and books were banned.

As I learned more, I realized I'd never even learned about the real history of Poland and the Second World War as a kid; the Communist regime falsified and twisted Polish history to suit their Socialist ideology. We were only taught how bad things were *before* the war and very little about what life was like for people during or after. In fact, there was more focus on teaching how great life was now, after the war and under a Socialist system. We never learned about wartime resistance efforts; we had no idea, for example, that the Polish government-in-exile (officially known as Government of the Republic of Poland in exile) and its military arm, the Home Army, was the biggest resistance movement in all of Europe during the war.

One of the greatest examples of the Socialist censorship and suppression of information is found in the story of Captain Witold Pilecki. In 1940, Captain Pilecki, one of the Polish Army resistance leaders, volunteered to allow himself to be captured by the gestapo in order to infiltrate the Auschwitz concentration camp. It was there that Captain Pilecki organized the resistance movement, which included hundreds of inmates. He created the report that was smuggled out detailing the horrors and atrocities occurring at the camp—this report made it into the Allies' hands, but it fell on deaf ears.

Captain Pilecki escaped Auschwitz and later fought in the Warsaw Uprising in 1944. He was a great Polish patriot and a great inconvenience to the Socialist regime in Poland. In 1947, he was arrested by the Communist state security police and charged with anti-Polish activities. He was then subjected to torture and a show trial. Captain Pilecki was officially executed by the Polish Socialist government in 1948, and was buried in an unmarked grave somewhere in Poland. Others would be sent to gulags or prisons across the Soviet Union, serving time as political prisoners. During Communist reign, Captain Pilecki's name was often whispered by the few who knew the story. He was feared by the

Communists, and ignored by much of the apathetic Polish society afraid to learn about the heroes of Poland. The Communist censorship of information regarding his story or that of other Polish heroes kept anyone from learning about these patriots and successfully erased and cancelled them from Polish society and history for almost fifty years.

As a result, years later, we had no idea these Polish heroes even existed. It was not until after Communism fell in Poland that Captain Pilecki, along with thousands of others, was fully exonerated and given the status of Hero of Poland. Some of their graves were never found, including Captain Pilecki's. Unmarked graves from the Communist regime were commonplace in Communist Poland and many other Socialist-ruled countries, and these graves are still being found today.

Suppression and disinformation came in so many different forms back then. And with the options for communicating with other people—your family, your neighbors, your community—being limited, the state was able to consume the rest of your time and attention with their messaging and their censored news. A person's time and attention are incredibly valuable, and this was when I learned not to take either for granted.

The government ordered the removal of all statues that didn't match their false historical narratives. Everything in our textbooks and literature was scrutinized for anti-Communist sentiment, then edited to remove it. Anything that could be warped to fit the Communist Party line got warped, until our sense of reality was almost completely skewed. It wasn't until the Soviet Union and Socialism collapsed in Eastern Europe in 1991 that a whole trove of history—full of countless horrible truths, as well as incredible stories of resistance, progress, and victory—was revealed to us and all the lies were exposed.

Like so many others in the party, my father would deny all culpability until the day he died.

★ CHAPTER SIX ★

STRIKE IT RICH

TO MY MOTHER'S DISAPPOINTMENT, I wasn't destined to stay in school for very long. Between a hard home life and a bleak future, I decided I might as well live my life rather than keep sitting behind a desk, absorbing information that wasn't even true. I wasn't getting any younger, after all.

This decision soon resulted in me and a few friends creating a smuggling ring of sorts.

In Poland, most people made the same or very similar amounts of money (with the exception of high-ranking party members and other political favorites). The government set the amounts; there was no arguing for a raise or anything like that, ever. But people needed to make ends meet somehow, even if the methods weren't exactly legal. Then again, even if a person made extra money, there wasn't much to spend it on. Communists liked to argue that food shortages happened because the Socialist economy was so strong, people had an extravagant amount of money and stores couldn't keep up with the demand. They said that empty shelves with no food and no goods were a good thing because it meant that Poles were rich...too rich. The Communists always claimed this as a sign of a strong economy.

Some of my friends from my taekwondo club and I decided we wanted to strike it big. No more sandwiches or pre-chewed gum—we wanted the big paydays, to go to places like Bulgaria, Russia, or Romania for a score.

We were put in touch with a girl from town who was very knowledgeable on the art of smuggling—or so we thought. She gave us the tricks of the trade (or some of them, anyways): First, we had to buy Levi's jeans in Poland and resell them to people in Russia. Second, we purchased hats in Russia and smuggled those to Romania, where fur hats were very popular at that time. Third, we had to sell the hats in Romania and with *those* earnings buy leather coats, travel with them back to Russia, and sell them there for an even steeper markup. To get to the end of this journey, we had to trade that Russian money for dollars, wrap those dollars up in plastic, and swallow the whole thing before hopping on the train back to Poland. Once home, we could retrieve the money and spend it however we liked.

On a good haul, I'd start with $80 and come back with $5,000.

But this process wasn't nearly as glamorous as it sounds. To sell the Levi's, we had to get them into the next country without getting caught. The solution: we'd wear as many pairs of jeans as possible at once. On one haul, I was wearing six pairs of jeans. I couldn't even bend my knees, and I had to be shoved up onto the train like a plank of wood. We would inevitably lose some stock during inspections—one guy got searched and was ordered to lift his shirt, which he did, exposing the absurd number of clothes he was wearing.

Once in Russia, we had to sell everything by hand as secretively as possible. We usually had to go into a random building to make the exchange—money for Levi's—so the police couldn't spot and catch us. And we sold everything—our entire supply would be gone except for the jeans we were wearing.

There was always another problem waiting around the corner on these smuggling jobs. Without a visa or other special papers, we couldn't officially stay in a Russian hotel. Luckily for us, it was good business for certain families to put up smugglers overnight. We would end up regularly staying in a single room with ten to twenty other smugglers. It was cramped and expensive and smelled to high heaven, but it was cheaper and easier than having to forge papers and stay in a hotel. That's not to say it wasn't scary or risky for those families to do what they did; they could have easily lost their homes and been shipped out to gulags while their kids were sent to orphanages. Most often, when caught, they were forced by the government to move to different cities deep inside the Soviet Union. But I think they recognized the need to do things differently than what the government wanted, and they wanted to support us however they could (and, of course, for the money).

To minimize the risk of getting caught, we'd wake up early in the morning and head out so we could mix in with the morning crowd going to work. This was a very eerie experience. Everyone was quiet, not talking, not smiling, dark streets without light poles, crowds of people walking in unison to work on both sides of the streets. This was January 1980, deep winter in the Soviet Union. It was so cold, and we'd leave so early in the morning that it was practically still night out. All I'd hear was the *crunch, crunch, crunch* of feet in the frozen snow. No one on the streets would look at each other. There were no cars. Some people took the bus, but most everyone kept walking. It was grim, shocking, and surreal to see and to know that this was people's regular existence. Compared to the noise of modern life, this was almost complete miserable silence.

We'd walk around this or that Russian town or city, always on the lookout for people selling the fur hats. Our leader, Johnny, who we gave the unaffectionate nickname "Crazy Horse" (he had a smile like a horse with giant crooked teeth and was basically insane), would carry nunchaku everywhere with him, and sometimes a samurai sword under his coat. We had no idea, and it never presented a problem, except for one visit to the Romanian border when we got caught with our surplus of fur hats. Johnny and the guards aboard the train were arguing back and forth about them taking half the goods, so the rest of us hid our bags on the train and waited for things to simmer down.

Once they did, we continued to Romania—Bucharest, in this instance—less one bag of product but ready to sell, sell, sell. Full of youthful vigor and generally lacking any self-awareness, we talked openly and excitedly about becoming millionaires. Johnny had to remind us: "You can't just walk out there and yell about selling this stuff. Be subtle."

I managed to sell my hats quickly. Pretty soon, I was thinking to myself *Holy shit, I* am *a millionaire!* Even if it was still a far-off goal, I'd never held that much money all at once in my life. It felt good, like I suddenly had options and could do anything I wanted with my life, if only I didn't live in Poland.

While we covered the whole town and sold off our supply of fur hats, Johnny had wandered off somewhere.

Even as we regrouped and prepared to return to the train station to head for Bulgaria, he was nowhere to be found. We looked around and quickly came across a huge crowd surrounding two crashed cars. Car accidents were very common at the time, so that wasn't particularly strange or upsetting. Once we pushed through the crowd, though, we found Johnny shoving his hand in the air over the shattered window, fur hat in hand, trying to make a sale to the other driver. Turns out, that's what had caused the accident, and Johnny's shouting had drawn the crowd.

Of course, once a crowd gathered, police were never far behind. They rounded up our entire smuggling crew, two cops per man, and took us to their outpost at the Bucharest train station. They quickly found Johnny's nunchaku and started beating him for it; they took that from him, along with the rest of his product and the money he'd already made. Fortunately, there was a truck that also delivered tons of bags of potatoes at the police station.

The whole time this was happening, people were coming in from one end of the (long) train station toward the center. There, one person per family would pick up a sack of potatoes from a station bench, then leave out the other side and head for home. There must have been fifty to sixty bags. It was at this time that the police became busy with the bags of potatoes and stopped beating Johnny up. We used this opportune time to pick up our own sacks of potatoes and leave, determined to disappear unscathed and eventually make our way to Bulgaria. We ditched our sacks of potatoes behind a corner at the first opportunity and ran. Since the police had robbed him, Johnny and a few other guys barely had enough money left, so we pooled our money to buy cigarettes there in Bucharest, go over the border to Bulgaria, sell the cigarettes there, come back to Romania with more money, and buy the leather coats as originally planned.

In the end, everyone but me went to Bulgaria to sell the cigarettes. I stayed behind, camping out in a hotel lobby in Bucharest and keeping watch over our mostly empty luggage (besides our own clothes, the empty space was reserved for smuggling the leather jackets). While I was there, two Romanian state security police dressed in plain clothes showed up, presented their badges, and started beating a Romanian citizen in full view of everyone. I could see the fear in the man's eyes, and I watched them beat him close to death and leave. Their victim eventually got up and hobbled home on his own, his eyes never straying from his own shoes.

I knew, given my uncle's experiences with the Communist regime and my father's tirades about Socialism, that this was a regular occurrence. The police could do whatever they wanted to anyone they wanted. There was zero accountability—under Communism, everything was sanctioned (if not ordered) by the government.

The other smugglers showed up the next morning with the money to buy coats. The plan was back on track! But we had one problem we hadn't accounted for: none of us knew anything about leather. Horse or mink or cow, it made no difference to me. I decided to go all in on a $350 girls' leather coat that I'd found and thought was really nice; I spent all my money on this one coat. Then we packed our bags and jumped on the train. This train, however, had no plans to make a full stop in Russia like we needed it to; it was scheduled to go straight from Romania to Poland. The plan was to jump off the train in Russia when it slowed down. That was a fine art in and of itself: there was a particular moment when we felt the train slow down, and we had five minutes max to disembark, while others on the ground had the same five minutes to climb aboard.

Our plan was to jump off the train, sell the coats, collect our money, trade it for dollars, roll the dollars into plastic, melt both ends of the plastic to seal it, swallow the thing, and get back on the train back to Poland—all in one day to keep the date entering and leaving the Soviet Union as the same day posted in our passports. Unfortunately, the plan changed yet again when I got sick on the train from Romania to Russia. Maybe it was from the drafty train, or maybe it was because I'd slept overnight in a chilly hotel lobby. All I knew was that I was freezing and miserable. I stayed at a stranger's house, huddled with my butt against a kiln to stay warm until I felt strong enough to venture out and sell my stock.

The problem with coats, of course, was that they couldn't just be handed out. You had to wear them so the police would not stop you for selling without permission. I put on the expensive girls' coat I'd been so excited about and immediately realized my mistake. It was so small, my arms stuck straight out and the bottom hem was up around my chest. I was a twenty-one-year-old guy and I looked like I was pretending to be a ten-year-old girl.

Everyone else was selling their wares except me. I just kept getting weird looks. The whole thing, I thought, was a bust: I was freezing, walking around aimlessly, and not making a single sale. Turns out the expensive coat I'd bought was tailored for a small girl and made of poorly tanned horse leather, which was like cardboard when worn. I looked like I was wearing an ugly umbrella.

Miraculously, three guys eventually came up to me and asked if I was selling. Four hundred rubles for the coat, I said. I was ready to give it to them. But we had to go to a hidden location to make the exchange to avoid the police.

We walked up three flights of narrow stairs, and I was on high alert the whole time. I knew the tricks—you show them the coat, he counts and holds the money (usually short of the asking price). He reaches out for the coat as you reach out for the money. You start counting and tell them, "It's short." You hand it back, then he counts it out again and agrees with you that "yes, it's short." He then looks at the other guy, telling him to give you the extra money. While you are looking at the other guy who is handing you the missing money, the first guy flips a prepared wad of newspaper cut to bill size into the stack and then hands it back, saying, "We're good now." Normally, it is at this point that the third guy at the bottom of the stairs keeping watch yells, "Police!" and they start to run.

I'd heard about a Polish guy getting killed in a deal gone wrong just like that the night before, and I was ready for their scam. However, I was happy with what they were giving me (only thirty rubles short of my asking price) and took the money not caring about what they were short; then I knocked the big guy out, ran down the stairs, and kicked the watch guy in the head. I kept running so I could get out before they tried to kill me.

But now I had to book it back to the train station, worried the whole time that these guys were looking for me. When I reached the station, I immediately went looking for as big a knife as I could find and sat with it up my sleeve, terrified. Worse, the train was just pulling out when I arrived at the station and now I was alone—all my friends, including Johnny, seemed to have already left for home.

After I missed the train, I wandered around the train station, checking on my options for catching a train home to Poland; I found my crew all sitting together. At first, I thought I had been mistaken and that they'd waited up for me after all. Turns out the police had caught them and took most of their money and merchandise, and now they were waiting for the same train as me.

But we weren't completely broke, which meant we could look for another smuggler's room for the night, and we still needed to buy drinks so we had something to help us swallow what little money we were left with.

Of course, we got into trouble on the way home. At the border, police came onto the train and tried to search our luggage, but we managed to shake them off. Then the other guy who'd swallowed cash got sick and had to go to the bathroom. What money he'd had in his stomach ended up all over the train tracks in Russia.

We got home eventually, tired, sick, and unsuccessful. I had to wash the money around fifteen to twenty times before I could count it.

I left home with $80 and came back with $90. I decided then and there that I would never try smuggling anything ever again. It simply was not worth it.

★ CHAPTER SEVEN ★

THE WORSE,
THE BETTER

THE COMMUNIST AND SOCIALIST HATE for America was pathological and so profound that all stops were pulled out in denigrating the United States as a country. You could hear it on TV, radio, and read it in newspapers and magazines. Even entire books were published disparaging America and US institutions. Most of it backfired on the Communists right away as some of it taught Poles how to defend themselves from Socialist perversion. The best example was a book published in Poland in the late 70s about the history of the Federal Bureau of Investigations (FBI) in which the author explained the technique purportedly used by the FBI to keep dissidents and inconvenient people irrelevant, terrorized, and in check. The author stated that the FBI used their informants, snitches, and people they had hooks in to spread rumors and lies about the dissidents who they preferred not to openly challenge or prosecute. The FBI purportedly spread these lies in the social circles of targeted victims. The victims knew nothing about it, at least not at the beginning. They only noticed that suddenly their friends started looking at them strangely or outright avoiding them. Their families often noted that their friends also abandoned them or distanced themselves. People and families purportedly targeted by the FBI lost job after job, and eventually were not able to find any work or friends. They often never learned what really happened. The victims' social standing was destroyed, and their influence on fellow citizens was often completely eliminated or at least greatly reduced. Books like those, describing the terrible tactics of a government out of control, were used by Communists and Socialists with the intention of painting the United States as an evil and oppressive state where fear ruled.

Unfortunately for the Communists in Poland, Poles never bought into the narrative that the United States was evil. We acknowledged that these tactics were being used, but not in the United States. What was described in that book was exactly what the state security police and other government services were using in Poland at that time. Poles who opposed Socialism were often outstanding citizens and could not be charged with fabricated claims; however, they suddenly found themselves and their families ostracized from their communities and circle of friends. The rumors were spread secretly, behind their backs, and the official Communist press was quick to "help" in the persecution by quoting some of the rumors to further push the isolation of inconvenient individuals and their families. It was a very effective technique used to silence the political opposition, especially to silence people that the Communists could not bribe or compel to cooperate.

An earlier attempt to discredit the United States, infamously known as the "potato beetle" story (or the "Stonka" story), had backfired on the Communists and Socialists in

Poland. In the late 1940s and 1950s, Warsaw Pact countries launched a propaganda operation that accused the United States, and the Central Intelligence Agency (CIA) in particular, of dropping crop-destructing insects from parachutes and balloons to cause famine in Poland and other Warsaw Pact countries! This was a synchronized propaganda effort by Communist Czechoslovakia, East Germany, and Communist Poland. In Polish news, most notably the now-famous newsreel from 1950 titled "The struggle against the beetle," they claimed that the entire world condemned the United States and American pilots of crimes for dropping tremendous amounts of potato beetles onto the fields of Poland and East Germany. Poles didn't buy into this narrative either. Even more so, the Communist narrative made Poles acutely aware of the inefficiencies of the Socialist economy and that even "Stonka" the potato beetle was kicking Socialist butt.

In their attempts to smear the United States with books and other propaganda, the Communist regime gave the people of Poland a tool to recognize and counteract these tactics. Poles learned very quickly to recognize and take note of people starting the spread of rumors. Poles started pointing them out as snitches and informants. The roles were reversed, and once a snitch was outed, their circle of friends and their influence waned very quickly, including the distancing of state security police who had been using these same agents, snitches, and collaborators. These informants quickly became pariahs among patriotic Poles. It was common for Communists and Socialists to try and extrapolate treason and the crimes of these informants onto the political opposition, but Poles had learned to dismiss these efforts.

Pope John Paul II paid the people of Poland a visit in 1979, inspiring the entire nation to rise up against Communist oppression and fight for freedom. His presence really raised people's spirits and morale. Of course, you wouldn't understand the impact if you only watched the government-controlled media. They tried to minimize his presence with edited images to make it seem as if only a few people were there; however, the number of people who showed up truly searching for hope was overwhelming. The visit awakened the Polish people's yearning for independence, and the Communists feared the aftermath of the pope's visit. He preached to us that we didn't have to live like slaves under this Communist regime. Hearing him speak was like breathing fresh air: there was so much propaganda coming at you all the time, it was hard to break through. Church became a refuge from the violence as much as the propaganda that incited it. It was the pope who told us, "Don't let people sway you with fear tactics."

There were plenty of ways to protest the oppression we faced in Poland. Some found ways to disrupt supply chains or the flow of capital, while others preferred brute force. My uncle, for example, besides being a cement manufacturer, was also a dump truck driver. The truck was owned by the government, but he was the operator. He'd regularly dump huge piles of dirt on workers' tools, which made the workers happy. Instead of having to perform heavy labor for a few dollars a week, they got to rest and collect the same pay. They were out to prove the dysfunction of the Communist state in whatever ways they could.

According to my father, a devout Communist, it was necessary to force people into Socialism. Many people did not appreciate the benefits of Socialism and the goals of

Communism. The government promised free this and that as a way to entice people to give up their faith and put their trust in the government instead of God. It was imperative for Communists to replace family values and morality with their own ideology. National Socialist Germany demonstrated this when Hitler was able to change minds into believing the holocaust was a moral thing to do; to euthanize less fortunate and ill people was the morally best thing to do. This is how dangerous relative morality is—it is evil and entirely without true morals.

Poland was a totalitarian Socialist police state. You had no rights, and if the Communist Party deemed you dangerous, you would be eliminated. My father always reminded me of this and was adamant that people who do not support Communism need to be purged from society, eliminated one way or another. Although these statements are very dark and dangerous, he was only restating what the Communist Party emphasized as the goals for society. Most people who knew my father would not think he is evil; he was a very loyal party member, but he was very gentle, very well spoken, and very well-liked by many, especially in the Communist circles.

By early 1981, after the Communist government raised food and fuel prices and lowered working wages, Solidarity had a membership of about ten million people and represented most of the Polish workforce. This is when my mom became involved with a trade union, and the first time in any Warsaw Pact country that an organization was formed independently from the regime, with real elections and everything. Through the union, strikes began, bringing entire industries to a halt. State-run companies were losing money, and they were deeply in debt to the West to boot. Desperate, the authorities tried to strike a deal with the unions. The agreement, at the end of the day, was to "allow" the trade unions to exist in exchange for fewer (if any) strikes. This was just a ruse in preparation for martial law to take down the first independent trade union of the Warsaw Pact.

Regardless, civil disobedience was rife, with lots of people constantly poking little holes in Communist logic and practices. Even if nothing came of it, we kept calling on the government to hold the elites accountable for their crimes—rape and stealing amongst the atrocities. The regime, however, would either claim there was not enough evidence to start an investigation or have a fake review of the crime and always come to the same conclusion—the elite Communist Party member was innocent. This was reiterated by the Communist-friendly media claiming that the elite member was "innocent," and that any further questions were only driven by hateful people with anti-Polish sentiment. It was not until the fall of Communism that many of these elites finally faced justice and many went to prison for their crimes.

At that point, I was more firmly entrenched with the anti-Communist Solidarity movement, and I'd regularly stay late at the headquarters in Lodz. Now that I was in my early twenties, I had a lot more flexibility to do what I wanted, within the constraints imposed by the regime, of course.

On December 13, 1981, around ten in the evening, people started coming in to tell us of their parents and other family members who were being arrested throughout the city. The state security police had come to their homes and their family members were gone. We knew that something big was about to happen. We braced ourselves for whatever was going to happen next. People started calling their friends in other countries outside of Poland, trying to organize routes of escape and chains of communication in case things went badly for us.

At midnight, I was on the phone with a taekwondo friend of mine based in Austria when the line suddenly went dead. Click. At first, I thought nothing of it—Socialist technology was inefficient and infamous for being faulty—but then others started coming in saying that their phones had been cut off. Turns out, entire phone lines had been disconnected across the country en masse. And as the phone lines, TV, and radio came down, the police began raiding homes and apartments and arresting people according to a list prepared earlier, leaving kids behind to fend for themselves. Guys I knew who had been out on the street having a smoke came back inside and reported that cops were raiding their apartments and taking away their families.

Someone at HQ turned the TV on, mentioning something about a government message being broadcast. General Wojciech Jaruzelski (who was really more Soviet than Polish) appeared on screen. He looked grim, in full uniform with the Polish flag looming over his shoulder. "The National Council, in accordance with the provisions of the constitution, has introduced martial law throughout the country," he read. "This is the last chance to pull the country out of crisis and save it from disintegration." Later, after the fall of Communism in Poland, it was determined that the martial law imposed by Communists was far from being constitutional, and perpetrators including General Jaruzelski were prosecuted.

He gave a whole speech about the constitution being suspended, that this action was for our own good; if the people obeyed the rules, he said, they would be safe. Jaruzelski stressed that Poland's government was on the verge of being overthrown, so in order to save the country, the government had to take drastic measures.

Police swept cities and villages throughout all of Poland based on their secret list. In my city, Communists arrested people in masses. They cordoned off the entire street where our HQ was based, creating a bottleneck and using it to arrest people. Inside HQ, militia members loyal to the regime were everywhere, trampling, beating, and arresting people. The building had been invaded, and everyone who the militia had on their list was taken to jail. Army tanks and armored vehicles blocked off the entire city, establishing checkpoints throughout. Military and police patrols, with the aid of the regime's state security police, were sweeping other towns, villages, and cities across Poland.

I somehow managed to get home, practically tiptoeing for seven miles in the cold and dark past the police. According to friends and other people I knew, TVs kept repeating General Jaruzelski's message. Meanwhile, people died because the phone lines had been cut and they couldn't call for emergency services. Others were killed outright by police or trampled in the panic.

As part of Jaruzelski's crackdown, media and educational institutions underwent "verification," a process that tested each employee's attitude toward Solidarity, which was outlawed the next year.

Thousands of people lost their jobs, and Solidarity leaders were arrested overnight. Independent-thinking artists, teachers, scientists, doctors, and others were silenced and cancelled and removed from the public eye. Full censorship and six-day workweeks were re-imposed, and the military quickly took control of coal mines and other industries. It is believed that over twenty-five thousand patriotic Polish citizens were arrested in one night on December 13, 1981. Varying sources list the number arrested between five thousand and sixty-five thousand. The Communist mantra was fed through the government-controlled media, which wanted us to believe that most of the arrested people were only temporarily held in the specially prepared internment camps created around Poland and that they were not really arrested. What Socialists called internment camps were just common prisons around Poland designated to house "interned citizens." The message the government was trying to convince us of was that there were no political prisoners and these people were not imprisoned; technically, they were only detained for their own safety and the safety of Poland. The government assured us that the internment camps were only there to protect the interned citizens from themselves. They quickly added that they could also be potentially dangerous to the Communist regime and their ideology. The key word is "potentially." This is how Socialism works. The main goal was to avoid the perception that the government held political prisoners. In fact, the government spokesmen said detainees had food, access to phones, bathrooms, everything they needed, but like so much of what came out of the Communist country during this time, it was all lies. Declaring martial law was just another attempt by the government to cull dissenters from the population.

When the president of the United States, Ronald Reagan, announced sanctions against the Communist regime on December 29, 1981, Poles, including myself, were cheering, even further infuriating Communists and Socialists.

This is when the phrase was coined: "Im gorzej, tym lepiej," meaning, "The worse, the better." It meant that the more sanctions put in place to ruin Socialism and Communism, the better for Poland, Poles, and freedom. Anything that even remotely hurt Communists was cheered by Poles. The Polish people were ready for any sacrifice just to get rid of the hated, oppressive Socialism that my father worked hard to put in place. After announcing the sanctions, President Reagan became the second most popular person in Polish society, after Pope John Paul II, and the most hated man on earth by Communists and Socialists. President Reagan was definitely my hero.

Those of us who escaped or were left out of the mass arrests met on the streets in the days following and discussed what we could do to resist this blatant show of terror and authoritarianism. The country was faced with news blackouts and total censorship, so we decided that it was important for someone to tell the truth of what was going on. We found one guy who had a typewriter and another who had a printing press, so me and a couple of my friends decided to report on what was happening on the ground. In the back of my mind, I kept thinking about what would happen if we got caught—being found with an unregistered typewriter, or God forbid, a printing press—usually meant spending some time in prison. My newspaper was really only a double-sided, single-page leaflet that we produced. But the messages it contained were dangerous enough that I could have been imprisoned. After printing a few hundred copies, we walked the streets of Lodz, pressing the uncensored newspapers into people's hands and leaving them in high traffic areas of the city, while desperately hoping one of the Socialist sympathizers would not turn us in. It was naive and we didn't know any better, but it was the only way available at the time to disseminate facts and the truth about Socialism, and to encourage fellow Polish citizens to resist the oppression.

Following the implementation of martial law on that night, December 13, 1981, in my city of Lodz, thousands of us would turn off our lights every month on the same day that started martial law to show solidarity against the regime. Whole city blocks would be completely dark except for a single candle in every window; twenty, thirty, forty apartment buildings all in a row, each twenty to thirty stories tall, each window with a candle in it. If you didn't see a candle in a window, you could assume the person living there was someone who supported or worked for the regime.

I'll never forget the sight. It was one of the most powerful and beautiful demonstrations, with the Poles showing solidarity with each other and against the regime in overwhelming numbers. It may not have had a larger political impact in the moment, but morale is important in times of struggle and oppression, and the sight of thousands of lit candles in the dark filled us all with hope.

During martial law—when symbols of the Solidarity trade union were outlawed as terrorist, anti-Polish, and disruptive—many people, including myself, started wearing American flag lapel pins in public as a symbol of freedom. The disdain for Communist and Socialist ideology only grew bigger every day. Communists and Socialists were losing their minds trying to understand why they could not make Poles hate America as an evil, racist terror state. The bottom line was that the Communist and Socialist propaganda was causing just the opposite effect. The Polish people always thought of America as the beacon of freedom and a country to be emulated and admired.

American symbols were thorns in the Communists' and Socialists' sides. In my city, Lodz, military and police patrols often stopped buses and trolleys at checkpoints where they would disembark passengers to check their documents. Those who normally wore Solidarity symbols were quickly hiding them...leaving only the American flag in their lapel. This always infuriated the Communists and Socialists. During one of these stops and document checks, they finally lost it. The police started ripping the pins out of our clothes, tearing off our jackets and coats. They collected quite a few of the American lapel pins, threw them on the ground, and started stomping and breaking them. That wasn't surprising to most of us, as we were aware of the Communists' hate and disdain for everything that symbolized freedom and America. My thin jacket's collar and left sleeve were almost completely torn off. Later my mom had to somehow sew it back together. After getting back on the bus and starting to pull away, one of the passengers yelled through an open window that we would buy more of them and wear them again. The bus was halted once more, and we were told to disembark. The individual that the police thought was smarting off to them was pulled out and "escorted" to the police patrol car, accompanied by curses, kicks, and rubber stick punches. I doubted that it was the same guy who had yelled—most likely he was just a random individual, one of the first and most convenient for the police to grab and haul out of the crowd.

Some resistance figures I knew quickly became very loud and outspoken, creating their own circles that people flocked to. New organizations were established every other day and just kept getting bigger and bigger. We didn't realize that some of these organizations were actually being established by the state security police (or with their secret support), who collected names and information and were then able to arrest opponents of Socialism in one fell swoop. The state security police infiltrated the leadership of a few other resistance groups and started sabotaging the message, poisoning our sense of solidarity from within, always with the insinuation *maybe martial law wasn't so bad...* (Everything came to light eventually, but it took years, and more is revealed every day thanks to organizations like the Institute of National Remembrance—Instytut Pamięci Narodowej (pl).)

Because my group was very small, no one thought to try and join us, let alone infiltrate us. We kept a low profile and covertly distributed our resistance literature out in the streets. I'm sure the police had been following us for a long time, but they didn't get anyone until early 1982, when I was walking toward the printing press down a tiny little street in Lodz. I happened to look up and noticed someone was watching me. He was maybe a hundred yards away and staring directly at me. Of course, I thought that was strange. But I kept walking and got to the building. I climbed the stairs to the third floor; suddenly I heard footsteps thundering over my head and a bunch of doors flying open. I had at least eight or nine guns pointed at my head. It really was like an old-school police standoff. They eventually got me on the ground and handcuffed me. I stayed down there with boots on my back next to my resistance friends, who were already handcuffed prior to me showing up. They waited for others to show up, but no one did.

The state security police hauled us off to their HQ that same night. They stripped me of everything except the clothes I was wearing and carried me off to a dark, smelly, cold prison cell. Even for all my troublemaking over the years, I'd never seen an actual prison cell up close. I'd only ever been in a holding cell. This was far worse. Reeking of piss and shit and mold, there were people huddled somewhere in the dark, but I couldn't see anything.

I stood there until someone called out, "Hey, you—just sit down somewhere." I had to feel my way around with my hands on the walls, blindly managing to find a spot on the wall among a dozen other people. Eventually, when they turned the lights on, I was able to see it was a small room with steel doors, with a raised "bed" in the middle that was more like a low pedestal a few people could lie down on at any given time. And there were food rations, but they were so small, I was soon painfully hungry.

Apparently, others were in a similar state. One prisoner, a real mean-looking guy, came up to me sometime after dawn and said, "I'm gonna eat your food today."

I wasn't about to give him the chance, not even a slim one—I knocked him out, and when he was laid out unconscious on the ground, I carefully lifted his upper lip and using my knuckles punched his two upper front teeth in to drive the point home: no one was going to mess with me in here. I pulled the knocked-out teeth from his mouth, put them in my pocket, and then ate his food.

Others in the cell asked me what I was in for.

"Solidarity."

This seemed to impress them. Nodding approvingly, one guy said, "We need to help you out, then."

Some of the men I shared that cell with were real nasty guys, but others were old salts—fundamentally decent men who'd lived hard lives. Those were the ones who showed me the ropes of how to survive and gave me extra clothes and food. Meanwhile, the guy who'd threatened me earlier and was now missing his two front teeth promised to spread my name at the big prison, making me a target by the time I got there. I told him if he did, I'd knock out his bottom teeth, too. I had his teeth in my pocket for a while, until they were taken away from me by the prison guards during one of the searches. I am not sure what ever happened to those teeth.

During my time at the state security police HQ in Lodz, I was interrogated anywhere from two to three times per day, where they asked me the same questions over and over. While imprisoned there, the police raided my apartment and destroyed everything. My mom and sister were not involved in my group; they were innocent the entire time, saying they'd picked up the literature—the pages my friends and I were producing illegally—off the street to throw away later.

The police told me they'd threatened my family. Their methods didn't work—as I stuck to my story, they tried different tactics and beat me with a heavy rubber nightstick for not confessing to their charges. My story was that I didn't know anything about a printing press, about resistance literature, anything. One evening, after interrogations were complete for the day, as they were taking me to another room, I saw a glimpse of my friend Jerry sitting there with his hands cuffed behind his back. Our eyes connected; he was shaking his head telling me that he said nothing. I let him know the same. He wouldn't say anything. I wouldn't say anything. We both knew what our job was: survive and deny everything. There is an old Polish thief saying: if they catch you red-handed, by your hand—deny that it is your hand.

As a result of our stonewalling, the police couldn't prove anything. Everything—the press, the typewriter—was being kept in this girl's house, someone we'd been working with and who kept up a false front to the police. Because we all stayed silent, they couldn't pin anything on any of us.

Regardless, they kept me there for three weeks, asking the same questions repeatedly, sometimes beating me when I didn't answer the way they wanted me to (or didn't answer at all). At the end of my stay, they announced they had everything they needed to put me in jail for life and that I was soon going to the big prison.

That same night, and without explaining anything further, the police marched me out at 2:00 a.m. in handcuffs. On our way out of their HQ, I saw that the guy whose teeth I'd knocked out my first night was still there in the communal cell. He looked rough. I didn't get a chance to ask him if he'd kept his word and told the guys at the big prison about me. The police kept moving, and under the cover of darkness they hauled me out onto the street and shoved me into the back of a civilian car.

"Where are we going?" I asked.

"When we get there, it won't matter to you anymore."

The thought crossed my mind that maybe they were going to kill me. I prepared myself to fight, getting my blood up while I sat handcuffed in the back seat of the car.

I knew it was a lost cause, but I would not go quietly. My plan was to hopefully knock out the two cops with a good kick when we got out, then make a run for it. It was naive, but I had no other option.

The whole time I was brainstorming, they drove. For almost four hours, in and out of town, over and over aimlessly until 6:00 a.m. when they brought me back to the cell at HQ. When I got back, confused by the change of plans and jittery from the adrenaline, I saw some of my cellmates were crying—they thought I'd been taken out and shot and they were the last ones to see me. They were sure they'd be next as the last people to witness me alive. Communism doesn't like witnesses.

When they saw me, they were so relieved. They offered me food and clothes, asking me what happened. This happened one or two more times. It was purely an intimidation tactic on the state security police's part, their attempt to try and scare the truth out of me. I was scared, definitely—I had plenty of fear, so much so I almost peed myself multiple times when these outings happened—but that fear didn't control me. I didn't respect these people, and that made all the difference. Having no respect for someone makes it easier to see through their bullshit, and very often, they know it too. But people who know they aren't respected often rely on fear to make up for it, as these cops did with their late-night joyrides. Regardless, my not respecting them made it possible for me to stick to my story.

When I was at last sent to prison in Lodz, most of my teeth had been crushed and chipped, and I was scrawny with hunger. But I knew the treatment where I was headed was not going to be any better.

CHAPTER EIGHT

LOCKED UP

FOUR WEEKS AFTER MY ARREST, I was transported to an intermediate prison in Lodz. The police investigation was done; now they were gathering materials and evidence to build a case against me. The absence of a confession or any proof was no obstacle for the Communist regime; if they lacked any evidence, they would make it up. But even though I knew they had a bunk case against me, I still didn't have an attorney to help me fight it. And going up alone against a corrupt justice system usually never ends well.

I was initially placed with common criminals, the worst of the worst violent criminals in a single cell. Some of them were snitches for sure.

The prison walls were made of concrete and reinforced with rebar. The whole place was cold and quiet; mold was everywhere. It was huge. The windows were very high on the walls with bars keeping us in and metal shields on the outside of the window preventing us from being able to look out. How many of us there were, and for what crimes (provable or otherwise), was anyone's guess.

The prison administration's intention was to break me down by putting me in the worst cell. The biggest guy of the group tried to strong-arm me into conforming to the cell's imaginary hierarchy of control. Of course, it did not end well for him. I applied a significant lesson I learned on the street: you finish the fight when *you* are done with the fight, not when he tells you he gives up. If you stop before submission, he could turn the tables and take you down. Despite this guy's screams to stop, I didn't. I kept beating him until he stopped screaming and stopped moving. He ended up with busted lips, two black eyes, and a broken nose. Unfortunately for him, there were others waiting to claim his position. As soon as he healed up, there were two others who beat him up, and he was no longer the leader of the cell. I started his downfall, and they never messed with me again.

The discomfort of prison can't be understated. Beyond the outright violence, there were millions of little things that made life miserable for all of us. One of those things was that you couldn't just lie in bed. You had to either sit down on the floor or on the stool, but you could not lean on the walls or the beds. There were four beds per cell (two bunk beds); however, it was not meant for the ten or more men that were actually in the small cell. When I'd first arrived, I didn't think much of it, and I was so tired and sore from my weeks at the state security police headquarters that I decided to lie down, even though the other prisoners told me I shouldn't. One of the prisoners said, "Don't do it or they will fuck you up."

"Screw that," I said. "I'm tired and I'm going to lie down."

My cellmates were smiling and smirking at each other in anticipation of what was to come. I ignored them and started to settle into the bed, preparing for some relaxation.

Sure enough, as soon as the bed—which was little more than a wooden cot—creaked under me, the guards came down on us. My resting time was up. They pulled me out of my new cell and started to work me over. I could hear their punches echoing throughout the prison as they landed on me. They beat me up and then threw me back in my cell.

When they were done with me, I thought for sure this time when I laid down, they would leave me alone. I was naive to think that because I could barely sit straight, they would surely leave me alone and let me recover in bed. It was not an act of defiance—not yet. However, it happened again, and this time they beat me with rubber nightsticks in such a way as to not leave too many bruises. This methodical beating included multiple hits to my kidneys, and I ended up pissing blood as a result. Once again, they threw me back in the cell.

This time, I was 100 percent sure that they were not going to mess with me. It was impossible for me to not lay down—I could not sit or stay standing—and so I went straight to bed. I thought they were going to leave me alone. I was wrong. They were not done with me, and the cycle repeated itself.

The third time is the charm, or so the saying goes, and it seems three beatings was the charm for getting the rest I was searching for. By this time, I couldn't see straight, my kidneys were bruised, and my teeth were chipped, crushed, and broken—I was swollen. At this time, I got really pissed. I was sore, and I hobbled to the bed and, just for the hell of it, laid down. I mentally prepped for another beating. The other guys sat on the floor and wouldn't even rest against the wall or the bed frames out of fear of the abuse they'd seen me suffer. The morning after what ended up being my last beating, I was still in bed and didn't get hassled for it. I think the guards—and the other inmates—thought I was crazy, but I really had come to believe there was no reason to keep beating me up, so I might as well be somewhat comfortable. I was naive, but miraculously, they left me alone. Maybe they looked at me and thought there wasn't much more damage they could do without killing me.

As a result of my one-man ignorance or perhaps resistance efforts (not so much defiance...yet), eventually one of the bigger, more prominent thugs in my cell decided to lie down, too. This was the same guy who had tried to push me around in the beginning, the guy who was supposedly "in charge" of the cell. I think he saw me doing it and thought, *You think you're tough? I can do it, too.* When he did, the guards rushed in and beat him up outside the cell while I was lying in bed. The guy was screaming bloody murder, and by the time they threw him back in the cell, he was dejected and only sat on the stool from then on. The only thing he said was, "I will sit," and I could not stop laughing.

I started to spend my time drawing on discarded newspapers left around the prison. One guy, a mobster, saw my work and noticed the awesome skull and crossbones I had drawn on a piece of paper. He wanted me to make a tattoo for him like my drawings. I had no idea how to create a tattoo on someone, so another guy made a needle and broke open a pen for the ink. Classic, old-school prison tattooing kind of stuff. The mobster wanted a tattoo of a skull and crossbones, he said. I decided to go for it—what did any of us have to lose—but it was so messy, and I could barely see what I was doing. When I finished, the guy had tears in his eyes, not because I'd tattooed a masterpiece, but because he was so embarrassed by what I had created, which looked more like a disfigured cow's head than anything. Definitely not a skull.

The mobster was horrified. "I'll get laughed out of the cell with this thing!"

He had to pay a bunch of cigarettes and other contraband to get someone else to cover it up with a vase and a bunch of flowers. It was a strange choice for a toughened criminal, but he liked it more than my attempt at a skull. That was my one and only attempt at tattooing while in prison. Even thinking back on that today, I still laugh.

The prison schedule for the day started with reveille at 5:00 a.m., followed by breakfast delivered to the cell at 6:00 a.m., and starting at 9:00 a.m. we had organized outside time. We would be marched outside, cell by cell, and never in the same pattern to prevent any potential collaboration between prisoners. While we were outside, we could walk about within a defined area for between fifteen and thirty minutes.

The holding tanks where we were allowed to walk were rectangular boxes, around twelve feet tall, thirty feet long, and twenty feet wide. The wall was made of reinforced concrete slabs that were slid between posts. They were not very precise, and the spaces between the slabs were filled in with cement.

One day when I was outside with my cellmates in one of the walking boxes, I heard the voice of Jerry, who was one of the co-defendants in my case, in the neighboring box. Jerry was a friend of mine, and I had seen him only briefly one time, when I was being marched to my cell from the interrogation room. I had not talked to him since the arrest. I knew these concrete slabs from my time practicing kicks with taekwondo on similar slabs. I used to break them in half. I thought if I could nudge it with a kick to create space between the slabs and knock out a bit of the concrete from the spacing, I would be able to see it was really Jerry on the other side. I jump-kicked a spot in the wall I'd already chipped away at, but instead of making a little peephole, the whole thing broke apart with a noise like thunder. The slab I kicked broke and fell out of the slots, and the slabs above it dropped like dominoes into the space. The alarms blared; guards rushed towards us. The prison special unit dragged me out and threw me in a separate cell until I was dragged back out for a meeting with the prison warden. My punishment for damaging prison property was two weeks of solitary confinement. My intention was not to break the wall, I only wanted to nudge it ever so slightly. I overestimated the strength of the wall, and perhaps underestimated the strength of my kick, and it caused chaos that resulted in me being sent off to confinement.

They took me to a cell that only had an open window covered by the shield that kept me from viewing outside but did nothing to keep the cold out. I was given a single thin blanket. They fed me water and bread on a regular basis, but nothing more. When my two weeks were up, I was sent back to my cell. What you need to remember is that the prisoners would rotate through cells frequently and it was never the same group in a cell for very long. We were moved at the convenience of the prison guards, and we were never with the same people for very long. So, when I returned to the cell, it was only a week later before I was moved out and into a new cell. It was there I met my first fellow Solidarity trade union member in prison for political offense charges like myself. His name was Edward Kędziorski. It was a real blessing for me to finally have someone I could relate to and that I did not have to fight. He stood by my side as I stood by his, providing encouragement to one another.

Edward was an experienced trade union member and very devout anti-Communist. He never tried to hide it or suppress his disgust with this oppressive ideology. His strength was an inspiration to me. We became good friends, and we are still good friends today.

Not long after, I talked Edward into training, mostly boxing, even though initially he hesitated, convinced we'd be beaten for it. I told him, "We can either sit here and get weaker, or get beaten up and get stronger." I started teaching him taekwondo and boxing; we passed the time shadowboxing, training, exercising, all kinds of stuff. Edward didn't know any martial arts before we started training together; he'd been a hard laborer who got caught protesting the regime, disseminating anti-Communist literature, and had received a four-year prison sentence for it.

Edward and I kept practicing, and after a short while he started to get pretty good at it. He was already a very strong individual intellectually, and I helped him become strong physically with our daily training. He was eventually moved out of our cell and transferred to another prison. It turned out that our practicing helped later on. In one of our conversations many decades after our release, he shared with me how the techniques we practiced helped to soften the blows and deflect the punches of the prison guards during one of his prison beatings, possibly saving his life.

With Edward being gone, some of my insecurities started to resurface. I felt alone again, not having someone to practice with or someone who I could share my ideas with for gaining Poland's freedom from Communism.

Eventually, a newcomer to our cell, a common criminal who thought a lot of himself and his fighting skills, asked to see what I could teach him. I told him, "I can show you something," and I had him hold his hands in front of him. "I'll show you a side kick, against the backs of your forearms." The guy didn't realize what was going to happen—he busted his own lip open with his own fists when I kicked him, and the force of it sent him flying backward. He hit his head against a cell door, and the sound carried far. He knocked himself out with his own fists and fell asleep into a deep stupor. When he came around again, he attacked me and tried to fight me because his ego was hurt. I had no option but to knock him out again. This time, he fell asleep so soundly that the rest of us in the cell became worried that he might die, so we called the guards over. He was taken out of the cell, never to be seen again. I was hauled out of the cell too, and waited once again for my meeting with the prison warden. Word spread quickly that I wasn't someone to be messed with.

I was given a week of solitary confinement once again, but this time it was in the so-called "tiger cage." For a moment I wondered if there was an actual tiger in the basement of this prison, but that was short lived. When they walked me into the cell, I burst out with laughter. It was so surreal! Within the cell room, they did indeed have a real cage. It looked like a very large dog kennel. They could not understand what was so funny, and my finding humor in the absurdity of the situation did not endear me to the prison guards. It was so odd to see this misplaced "tiger cage" within the walls, a cell within a cell. The cage had steel bars as big as my thumb and a low clearance so I couldn't stand upright. My only two options were to sit or lie down on hard steel. They tossed me in and my week started.

I didn't hate solitary confinement. Not completely. It was cold, dirty, and dark. It smelled, and the only light in the room was always flickering or completely dark. I only had a tiny blanket and a little wooden slat for a bed, but at least I didn't have to deal with the other prisoners, or the guards for that matter.

I spent only a few cold and uncomfortable days in solitary confinement before the prison guards came in. I thought they would just send me back to my cell.

To my surprise, they instead said, "We're putting you on a transport."

That gave me pause. "Where am I going?"

"Russia, maybe. We don't know."

Leaving the Lodz prison was not nearly as dramatic as when I left the state security police's headquarters. There was no one to watch me go; the guards hauled me out and put me onto a prisoner transport without another word. There's no denying, even now, how scary that was. And when I settled into the back of the transport, I realized the other guy was none other than Jerry, who I'd gotten arrested with. He was sitting across from me. We talked under our breaths, and I learned from him that while we'd both stuck to our stories and kept our secrets safe, the woman whose apartment we'd been using as a base for production had gotten arrested and had her children taken away, threatening that she would never see them again if she did not cooperate—she cooperated.

Neither of us blamed her for our situation or resented her for her choice. The Communist regime would go after entire families without hesitation if they thought they posed a threat; being a single mother, it was understand-able that she did what she thought she had to do to keep her children safe.

We were taken to Hrubieszów, a political prison on the Russian border. It was so close we could literally see the border through the prison bars. When the reality of where we were set in, fear started to spread. What would happen to us, we wondered, if the Russians invaded to "calm" the situation in Poland and take over? The Russians knew bet-ter than anyone that if the Poles got away with taking down Communism, the rest of the Eastern Bloc, including the USSR, would collapse as a result. This would bring down the entire Warsaw Pact. And that is what eventually hap-pened. Poland was the first country to kick out one of the bricks from the wall of totalitarianism, and this started the crumbling of the wall, which resulted in full collapse of Communism decades later.

Hrubieszów was a totally different prison from Lodz. It was classified as one of the harshest prisons in Poland. The prisoners were separated by blocks with the common criminals being in a different location from the political prisoners. Prisoners also had more opportunity to inter-act with other like-minded prisoners. It also became a very educational environment as we were sitting in prison with many intellectual members of the Polish society: doctors, professors, physicists, economists, and engineers, as well as other hard-working Polish patriots. We all shared the same disdain for Communism and Socialism.

The cells here were larger, the time allowed outside was much longer than at my last prison, and the food was better. Some of the prison guards did not hate or show disdain for the political prisoners. In fact, they often felt sorry for us and were uncomfortable keeping us in prison. These were fellow Polish country men from all walks of life; some were local farmers, and many were just trying to make an extra buck to feed their families. They were in this far outpost, often sharing similar disdain for the Communist regime.

The prison was on the Russian border near the town of Hrubieszów, where many of the town residents also shared the same sentiments towards the Communist government and oppressive Socialist ideology. A priest came every Sunday and was allowed to conduct Catholic mass for the prisoners. This helped us survive—it riled some people up and made them emotional because they had been cut off from their faith when Communism became the law of the land decades before.

One of the routines at Hrubieszów was to open the windows at 8:00 p.m., and the entire prison sang patriotic Polish songs that the state hated. Every night, entire prison blocks joined together in singing songs about freedom and independence. These songs carried into the small town and beyond. The local Polish population liked to hear this patriotic resistance. The guards tried to squash it, dragging prisoners away from the windows, but we persisted as there were not enough guards to stop all of us and our determination was strong. In a cold, lonely place like that, morale was vital for our collective survival.

☆☆☆

As a prison for political enemies of the state, the population wasn't just made up of young strong guys like me; there were older men, fathers and grandfathers, who never committed any crimes in their life but who had resisted the regime in small ways or didn't do things to the Communists' satisfaction. They lived in fear for their lives as well as their families' lives, yet they persisted. This kind of oppression didn't just affect the prisoner—it affected everyone they knew and loved, and that was an entirely different level of fear. It was common practice for the Communist regime to attack and harass the entire family of political dissidents.

I was thrown into a prison cell with Andrzej Krasuski and three other men. Andrzej was an engineer, from the city Bełchatów, and leader of the opposition there. An expert historian, Andrzej knew the history and literature of Poland on a very detailed level. He was also a natural born leader with very strong convictions. I remember him as one of the most respected and influential political prisoners in Hrubieszów. Andrzej used his skill to educate his fellow prisoners on Polish history—the real Polish history that the Communist regime worked so hard to censor, twist, and lie about. Before John Paul II's second visit to Poland, when the Communist regime relaxed the terror somewhat, Andrzej organized courses of Polish history and literature for all the political prisoners in Hrubieszów. Andrzej, through his strength and his leadership, helped me and many other political prisoners to survive the prison time. We remain good friends today.

Although some of the guards were understanding of our situation, there were other guards with a similar mindset to the animals at my last prison who were eager to show their sadistic inclinations. One day, before a medical checkup, the guards who'd come to collect me decided to beat me and two other political prisoners: Tadeusz Podlasek and Janusz Sijka until we were bruised and bloody, for no real reason other than they could. When the rest of the prisoners found out about this random display of violence, the prison went on strike. Prisoners were banging on the doors and window bars until the prosecutor and inspectors were called in. A few days later, the warden was fired and lost his job.

AUGUST 13, 1982

We started a hunger strike for the recognition of our status as political prisoners. The regime had been hiding and denying for decades that they held political prisoners. The last thing they wanted was to admit that the Socialist state was holding political prisoners, especially at such a volatile time in Polish history. Instead, their propaganda was to show us all as being criminals who committed common crimes.

After a certain point in our hunger strike, once we'd wasted away a bit, the guards started to force-feed us per the prison regulations. They would drag us into separate rooms in the medical unit and tell us we had a choice: they could shove a pipe down our throats and force-feed us, or we could eat and swallow on our own. Either way, we had to eat. Most of us stuck to our guns and said no.

That wasn't what they wanted to hear.

The feeding procedure was to bring the prisoner in, strap them to a wooden chair, and shove a corrugated feeding tube down the throat. It looked more like a vacuum tube than a feeding tube; it seemed way too big to be a medical feeding device. They would push the pipe down your throat and deep into your stomach. Using a funnel, they would dip a large jar into a deep vat of yellow sludge that was then poured through the funnel and into the tube.

First, they tried to do it to us in groups, but when enough people resisted, they started doing it one by one. This was a strategic move on their part. It was easier to talk to someone one-on-one and reassure them that "no one else will know," lulling them into a false sense of security. Their method was to convince a prisoner to take the cup for sludge and drink it himself, instead of them having to shove a thick pipe down the prisoner's stomach, and having that sludge poured through a funnel.

It was a trap—the moment after someone took the cup and drank from it, they were immediately informed that taking that sip on their own meant their hunger strike was over, then they were separated from the striking population and eventually removed and sent to another prison. At that time, the farther away from home you were taken, the less likely it was that you would be able to communicate with others.

The first time I was taken in for the procedure, I was strapped to the chair like everyone else, but when they started to shove the pipe down my throat, I panicked. It was so painful and invasive, I fought back. I broke the chair to pieces and continued to resist. The guards held me down, pried my mouth open, shoved the pipe in, and poured the putrid solution down. Many of us eventually learned how to deal with this feeding and get through it without any issues, and our protest continued on.

In the meantime, the Catholic priest was banned from conducting mass for political prisoners. On his own, risking his freedom, he came to the wall of the prison along with local parishioners and conducted mass in the field close enough that we could see, hear, and participate. To the prison guards, it was a threat. To us prisoners, it was another huge morale boost—the priest was risking so much to do something like that, flouting the regime and performing mass out in the open to political prisoners of the state. I was in awe of him. I wish I knew his name because he was largely responsible for my returning to church later on after my release.

I don't even know how much I weighed when the other hunger strikers and I decided to apply to be considered political prisoners, officially. We sent a letter to the head of the Polish Catholic Church; the response we received was to stop the hunger strike immediately. "The Socialist totalitarian government would rather die than list you as political prisoners," we were told. Hungry and at a loss, we ended our hunger strike, but we were determined to keep up our resistance in other ways.

It was around this time that my mother came to visit—visitors were allowed once a month, if they could make it all the way out to Hrubieszów. The first thing she said was that she was very proud of me.

"Of course you are," I replied. "For what?"

She then showed me a letter she'd received from the prison warden that said I was disobeying rules and generally being a problematic prisoner for them. Their expectation was that my mom would come to visit and persuade me to change my ways. My mother grinned as I read the letter, but she was fussing over my skinniness a moment later. I wasn't the same young man she'd seen only two months before, prior to our hunger strike. I was thin and looked like I'd barely slept, because I hadn't. The mental toll of being in prison was nothing compared to the physical toll, and I was feeling both. My mother, despite her pride in me, was afraid for me and our family. Eastern European Socialist regimes were well known for not only terrorizing the opponents of Socialism, but their entire families as well. The terror was not limited only to the offender. This also expanded beyond the direct family members to the extended family members, friends, and coworkers, who also became targets of the Socialist terror state. Sometimes it was enough that if the wrong person in the line for bread heard you criticizing the government, they would notify state security police who would then bring the wrath of the Socialist state upon you, your family, and friends. It was truly Orwellian—in fact, the book *1984* was forbidden in Poland at the time.

It was a grim, remote place to be imprisoned. Despite being staffed with some really awful people, not everyone in the prison administration was bad. Some of the nurses were especially great—a few of them had been part of the Solidarity trade union before they were press-ganged into working in the prison system. One nurse, I remember, even snuck us what was essentially rubbing alcohol to drink on Christmas. It tasted foul, but it did the trick, and it was as good a Christmas as any I'd ever had.

★ CHAPTER NINE ★

EYES OPENED

THE COMMUNIST REGIME IN POLAND, following another visit from Pope John Paul II, announced amnesty for prisoners including political prisoners like myself. In Poland at that time, people always tried to dress decently, even if they were poor. When I left Hrubieszów in the spring of 1983, I was smothered in my old winter clothes, which hung off my starved frame like a costume. And for all the production behind my arrest and imprisonment, in the end, the guards at Hrubieszów basically kicked me out via the front gate and said, "Off you go." That was it. Besides giving me my old clothes back, they also gave me just enough money for a train ticket home, but I had to walk all the way to the train station in my old winter clothes and heavy boots. Some passersby pointed at me and whispered, laughing behind my back, calling me a bum. I was freed from prison, but not a free man…not yet. I arrived home that same night and was so happy when my mother put real homemade food in front of me. She certainly got no protest or resistance from me.

Even though I managed to get out of Hrubieszów, its presence in our lives was unavoidable. The regime kept some of the prisoners I spent time with behind bars for years, well after most of us left. The men who didn't have families to plead their case or give them some hope for life on the outside suffered the most. And even as the guards at Hrubieszów were dealing with their inmates, the police in Lodz and all across Poland were busy terrorizing whole neighborhoods, threatening people with the possibility of being thrown into a place like Hrubieszów as a way to keep them in line. I don't know if party members or the larger regime knew this (I imagine they did), but by 1983, the people were so tired of the hunger, terror, and years of fear they endured under the Socialist state that they were ready to hang Communists from the lantern posts if they could have gotten their hands on them.

The regime must have known it, at least a little bit, because as the first cracks in the regime slowly started to appear and as their fear of the Polish people grew, there was a concerted effort among Communist groups to try and get people to cooperate. Communist agents infiltrated the intelligentsia as well as anti-Communist organizations, doing everything from carefully spreading misinformation to beating people up with no repercussions to sow discord and confusion. They would disrupt legitimate protests by embedding themselves within the protestors, instigating violence by attacking other protestors or even the police. They also instigated small terror groups, which were built from poorly educated or Marxist indoctrinated young men who were easy to influence. The groups were used to terrorize people opposing Socialism around Poland. The Communist government worked with their complicit media to try and convince the people that these groups were only concerned citizens with good intentions trying to protect Poland from Fascism and Nazism. We were used to the Communist lies, and we all knew these groups were supported by the regime and not spontaneous protests by good people in Poland. In reality, these terror groups of thugs and bandits operated under the patronage of the Communist Party, allowed to and even paid to bring violence to Polish patriots and anyone who opposed their leftist ideology.

Those efforts reached a climax when three state security police agents murdered an openly anti-Communist Catholic priest—a man named Jerzy Popiełuszko—in October 1984. He was speaking publicly about freedom and the importance of not living on your knees. He inspired other Poles to speak their minds and hearts and not to fear the Socialist terror. Popiełuszko had been targeted by the regime for years; they'd tried to discredit him as a religious leader, frame him for running guns, all kinds of things. But when nothing stuck, they murdered him.

The Communist Party's ability to silence Polish society for so many years via censorship and infiltration efforts was powerful, but it wouldn't last forever. However, in the moment, we struggled to see through to the other side of their oppression. (Like so many aspects of this history, none of these facts came to light until the Institute of National Remembrance revealed a trove of classified information in the late '90s and early 2000s. It was also how we learned that many of our anti-Communist leaders turned out to be informants living among us.)

We continued to live under the cloud of Communism, fearful but determined to see ourselves through to liberation. But the threat was alive, and it was everywhere—if someone so much as mentioned "Socialist elections," they could be arrested, even disappeared. We called these elections "Socialist elections" because the Communists and Socialists—through fraud, terror, and intimidation—always won. Elections weren't public, after all; "ballots" were counted in secret and "elected leaders" were announced. We had no say in our elections whatsoever. But eventually, the terror tactics of the state gave way to the people's underground networks, our uprisings, our protests, our voices.

After I was released from prison, I became hyperaware of the Communist atrocities being committed and the miserable living conditions in Poland. I was embarrassed by how long it took me to realize how bad it was and had been for years. I blame ignorance and naivety, and at least I realized it eventually, but it was hard to see the truth with the powerful censorship and propaganda of the Socialist state. And it was ironic because I had been living in such similar circumstances to those around me, but it wasn't until I ended up in prison that I began to meet more people from different walks of life who'd suffered even more than I had. They taught me to look beyond myself and to take other people's experiences into consideration, because even under Communism, plenty of people suffered more than others.

And that priest, Tadeusz Pajurek, who'd regularly visited Hrubieszów to perform mass for the inmates? He really did inspire me to become more in tune with my faith after I left, reconnecting with religion and God. I think I had to *see* the worst in order to believe the worst. Before that, when I was younger, I hadn't been able to really *believe* any of it, even though I knew my family was worse off than others and I could see families who were worse off than mine. The propaganda was so prevalent and convincing, the realities of our national dilemma were distorted to the point that the truth sounded more like conspiracy theories than fact. And then I ended up in Hrubieszów, far from everything I'd ever known, surrounded by other political prisoners who'd lived very different lives than me, but we all had prison in common. And prisoners don't have much else to do besides talk to each other, so that's what we did. We talked, and I learned.

In our discussions, religion came up a lot as well. The combination of those conversations with the other inmates and the visiting priest turned religion into a form of hope for me. I started listening to the message and to what people prayed for and realized it wasn't just about faith but about hoping for something better in life: freedom from oppression.

At home, my mother and grandmother were delighted when I started going back to church, because doing so didn't just mean I was finding hope again—I was actively spitting in the face of the Communist regime. The Socialist state and Communist Party spent a lot of time, effort, and resources trying to degrade the Church, faith, family, patriotism, and people's moral compasses. The Communist regime believed that depravity and perversion, when thrown on society, make it easier to divide people and therefore control them. Relative morality was key. For Communism to succeed, your morality must be based on the ideology and the political agenda of those in power, not on God's laws. God gave faith and strength to people, which made them dangerous to the regime.

★ CHAPTER TEN ★

LEAVING POLAND

EVEN THOUGH I'D BEEN FREED from prison, I was still considered an enemy of the state. Maybe not a particularly dangerous one, but an enemy nonetheless. After I returned home, I was a frequent victim of random psychological and physical attacks from the state security police. The state security police and Communist officials kept me on their radar. They often stopped me on the street and forced me into their cars. I was forced to ride in their cars for hours while they threatened to make me disappear, until they finally stopped and told me to get out. Under constant surveillance, I feared I would join the many political activists who had suddenly vanished or were suicided. I heard about unmarked graves in the Katyn Forest, where the Soviet state security police executed thousands of Polish nationals in 1940. Even today, Poland is still uncovering many graves of opponents of Socialism from 1945 through the late '80s.

It never escalated to the point that I faced prison time again, but it was a constant fear, and it became impossible to live my life. Trying to live normally when you're regularly looking over your shoulder, waiting for some state security police officer to jump out of the shadows or from around a corner, isn't life. It's torture.

I lasted for only a few months. In the autumn of 1983, I finally decided to visit the US embassy in Warsaw to request political asylum and ask for help. While there, I explained everything that had happened to me and was still happening to me. There were people who had been in prison that were murdered or disappeared, and I didn't want to find myself in their position. My visa was approved within a month of that visit, but I still had to jump through a ton of hoops, visiting various government offices to prove that I was in good standing, wasn't eligible for the draft, and more besides. Simply put, the state tried to make it as painful and difficult as possible for me to leave the country.

When I went to the Polish military's headquarters for visa clearance from the draft, the officer on duty yelled at me with spit flying from his mouth, saying, "People like you shouldn't be leaving this country! They should be staying and serving this country under the Polish eagle!" pointing his finger to the eagle emblem hanging on the wall behind his desk. (Ironically, his title was "recruiting officer," even though recruitment wasn't an option at that time—service was mandatory unless you had a record like I did.)

I quickly pointed out to him that the eagle was missing his crown. I instructed him that the eagle behind his desk was not Polish at all—it was the Communist version of the eagle with the crown removed so as to not offend the Communists with royal symbols. "The real Polish eagle was sent to the gulag in Siberia after the war. Your crownless eagle does not represent the people of Poland. The crown was stolen by the Bolsheviks, Communists, and Socialists. I would never serve under this imposter, and I do not wish to be in your shoes or those of any Bolshevik lackey when Poland's real eagle finally returns," I stated firmly. He didn't like that. I could hear the shouting and stomping of this Bolshevik goon as I was leaving the office and walking onto the street with the papers that would allow me to leave Poland.

In the end, party officials refused to give me my passport until I purchased $10 to $25 in United States currency. While $10 to $25 isn't much to us now, for Poles at the time, it was so much that I had to borrow some money from my mother to exchange for the other currency to make the payment. I went to the US embassy again and finally, *finally* got my visa approved and stamped.

The relief was instantaneous and incredible. I felt like a king. As I walked home to tell my family, all I could think was, *I'm leaving this treacherous place!* I can't even think of the exact words to describe the feeling. It was like I was walking on air and could breathe freely for the first time in my life. It was mixed feelings for my mother who was happy that I would be safe and living as a free man; however, she knew that it meant we may never see each other again. The passport provided was a one-way passport only for leaving Poland. It specifically stated that I could cross the Polish border only one time.

I understood my mom's fears and shared her concern that I might not ever see her or my family again, but I had no choice. It was either stay and possibly be murdered by the Communist government or have a chance for freedom and safety from Socialist oppression.

When I walked onto the plane that would take me away from Poland, I was twenty-three years old and only had a duffel bag full of clothes and basic toiletries, the $25 I'd purchased, and the life experience to give me the confidence to look the future in the eye and say, *I'm ready for whatever comes next.*

West Germany was the first stop on my journey to freedom. Before we landed, I was instructed by the plane crew that someone would meet me at the airport and help prepare me for my life in America. Because it was such a long distance from Poland to the US, it was easier to chop up the journey into sections. That way, I could await entry into my new country in safety and not in Poland where I was constantly in danger. In Germany I learned a lot from American citizens and Polish ex-patriots living there who worked for the US State Department and were assisting me and other Polish political refugees in the transition to our new life in America. They taught me and others fleeing from various oppressive Communist terror states what America is like, the customs, social mores, and how to be successful by being good American citizens. It was a lot to learn, and even then, it barely scratched the surface. There wasn't any time for us to learn English while in Germany, but they assured us that we'd pick it up.

This is when I made a promise to myself that I would be the best citizen that America could have. It was my pledge to America, the greatest country in the world—the land of the brave and land of the free.

Eventually, they asked each of us if we had a preference as to where we'd like to be relocated and settled once we got to America. I immediately asked to be sent anywhere that was hot. After twenty-three years in Poland, I was so sick of the cold. They decided to send me to Memphis, Tennessee, which I knew nothing about other than that Elvis was from there. I said, "If it's hot there, then it sounds great!" When the time came, I left Germany for Memphis, excited and restless with a bit of stressful curiosity for the adventure that lay ahead.

On March 21, 1984, I landed safely, albeit exhausted, in America with the equivalent of ten US cents in my pocket. I was picked up from the airport by a church family who'd volunteered to host me while an apartment was being set up.

That part didn't take long at all. Within days of my arrival, I was brought to my new apartment near the projects in downtown Memphis and was completely stunned. It wasn't the nicest place, but it was mine, and most importantly, it was in America. For me it was the most beautiful place on earth. The fact that I suddenly had an air-conditioning unit, central heating, and a refrigerator was mind-blowing to me. Growing up, I'd always thought those big white boxes in American windows were ice chests being used similarly to how we would store food that needed to stay cool by placing items on the ledge outside of our windows in Poland. When I saw these units in American movies, I was impressed with the American ingenuity of keeping the food in boxes to prevent it from falling off the ledges. It turns out, they were air conditioners! I was very proud of— and excited by—these developments. I couldn't wait for the people who'd brought me to the apartment to leave so I could use my new telephone to call my mom and tell her about the place. Having a telephone in my own apartment was a novelty itself, as it was extremely uncommon to have phones in apartments in Poland at the time. If you did have one, it was often shared by many other families within the same building to avoid having to run to find a phone booth.

This is how my life in America began.

My first job was as a janitor at a local church, cleaning toilets, floors, and windows. I couldn't contain myself when they gave me my first paycheck and I realized that I could afford to pay for my own apartment. I was ecstatic! Parishioners from my sponsor church bought me an English dictionary to help me build my language skills; they also offered to drive me around Memphis to get a sense of my new surroundings, to which I eagerly agreed.

I was sitting in the back seat of the car saying English words out loud while we drove around, using this new dictionary to make sentences and identify objects, and the couple, an elderly husband and wife, sat in front.

"Tree."

"Yes!" they would confirm with excitement.

"Woman."

Learning new words in a new language, seeing all these new sights—I was so excited I felt like a little kid on a ride at an amusement park. The next time I looked out the window, I saw a Black man walking down the sidewalk. I looked at the dictionary I'd been given to try and find the word to describe him.

The word I found and used was definitely not the right one—when I said it out loud, the driver almost wrecked the car, he was so shocked. His wife turned around in the passenger seat to look at me, horrified.

"Who taught you that word?" she asked with exasperation.

I wasn't sure how to respond and simply pointed to the "n" word in the dictionary they had given me.

She asked for the dictionary from me, took out a pen, emphatically crossed out the word, and replaced it with the correct and more acceptable term, "Black man."

I'm so glad she corrected me. I still have that dictionary today. You see, race was a very different conversation in Poland when I was growing up. We didn't make distinctions back then as Polish society was mostly Caucasian, with some Romani families, which were few and far between. We all looked the same, so there were no distinctions to be made. I never even met a Black person until I was eighteen years old. There were only the two Black karate students that I knew, who came through Poland; I trained with them, and I thought they were cool. They were new students who were very interested in learning martial arts and were there for only a year or so. We fell out of touch after they left, but we were good friends while they were with us.

But in Memphis, I was amazed to see people of all colors everywhere. And a lot of them were just like me—immigrants, asylum seekers, refugees. They came from Eastern Europe (Eastern Germany, Czechoslovakia, Romania, Bulgaria, and even the Soviet Union) and Cambodia and Vietnam. They came from everywhere seeking freedom from oppression. Regardless of where we'd come from or what we looked like, we were all connected by our desire and determination to carve out better lives for ourselves in America.

I had a lot of respect for the immigrants I met in Memphis. I'd be leaving for work at 6:00 a.m. and I'd see a lot of them only just getting home from working overnight shifts. And while there was some crime in our area, compared to what I was used to, I wasn't worried about it. Plus, I knew I could defend myself and others if necessary.

To help alleviate some of my residual fears—memories of being harassed and attacked whenever I walked out my door in Poland were still fresh—I decided to start exploring Memphis. I didn't have a driver's license, so I did what I did best: I walked. Everywhere. Which was normal for me but was apparently very out of the ordinary to the people of Memphis. I'd be out walking along roads and highways, enjoying the exercise and the sights, and multiple people would stop and offer me rides or directions. Even the police! That was an interesting moment for me. When I explained what I was doing, people were very confused. But I was so used to walking I didn't see an issue with it, even if there weren't any sidewalks to use.

It was during one of these excursions that I discovered that instead of a downtown area like I was used to in places like Lodz and Warsaw, there were huge shopping malls where everyone went to shop, socialize, see movies, play arcade games, and whatever they could think of. We knew nothing about malls in Poland. We didn't even know they existed. The first time I walked into one, I was stunned, and I ended up spending hours there just wandering from store to store, amazed by all the things people could buy and do all in one place.

I was truly so impressed by the Americans I met in Memphis. In those early days, I couldn't afford much in the way of food or basic necessities; the church gave me food and community when I needed both of them the most. My neighbors and the people I met through work welcomed me with open arms. They didn't judge me for where I was from or for the fact that I couldn't speak English or drive. The other immigrants and I were close, too, living side by side, working and striving together to earn our place in the country that had granted us a second chance at life.

Recently, my family and I drove past my very first apartment in Memphis. It was surreal being there again with the perspective I have now. The building itself has been condemned, and there are very few houses near it that have anyone living in them. We drove through at twilight, and I had a very anxious yet excited feeling with my wife and children in the car. I wanted to share the beginning of my American dream with them, and yet it was not much to look at anymore. Even when it was filled with people and activity, I suppose it wasn't much to look at, but it gave me a sense of pride and hope for what I had accomplished and would be able to accomplish living in a country with so much opportunity.

CHAPTER ELEVEN

AMERICA THE BEAUTIFUL

NOT LONG AFTER I FIRST arrived in America and was still getting my bearings, some people from the church near my apartment building invited me to a family pool party. I was incredibly excited, both to go swimming and to attend my first official American party. But as would happen a lot in those early days, culture shock was right around the corner.

As the folks at this party would learn, in Poland, our swim "trunks" were actually very tight and very small (the smaller the better), so when I came out wearing what was colloquially called a "banana hammock" (two new words for me to learn), everyone was scandalized. I didn't know any better and wasn't bothered, but I also knew that I was the odd man out in this situation. I was quickly ushered away from the pool area in one direction while the children were ushered out in another direction. I was given a pair of large and long shorts and asked to wear them instead, especially around the families. I accepted the swim trunks to wear instead; although I'll admit I was indignant at first—long trunks are what old Polish men wear when they can't dress themselves or are obese—I put them on without argument.

The learning curve in America was very steep for me. Another example occurred when I was at an after-mass fellowship gathering. The parishioners of one of the churches wanted to introduce me to the local church community and formally welcome me with the opportunity for me to say thank you to everyone for the support. The problem was, in Polish, we don't pronounce "th" sounds, so words like "thank" and "this" and "that" were hard for me when I was just starting to learn English. Another Polish immigrant understood the challenge and advised me of a quick remedy. He told me it was one that always worked. He recommended that any word spelled with "th" be pronounced with an "f" sound. If you say it very quickly, no one will notice, he told me. So, when the time came to thank these people for hosting me, I unfortunately was not quick enough with my "f" and it came out sounding like "f*** you" instead of "thank you." The fellow immigrant who gave me the advice was standing behind the parishioners and quickly disappeared. Another kind church member stepped in and said, "What I think he is trying to say is 'Thank you,'" to which I nodded my head very strongly.

With a mop in one hand and a dictionary in my back pocket, I navigated my new world cautiously and curiously. I wasn't used to being around people who looked me in the eye and said hello and meant it. For the most part, I kept my head down and my attention on my own circumstances. It honestly took me a long time to realize that not only had I made it to America, I was here to stay. That sense of permanence took a while. Once it did, I dedicated myself to being the best American that America could have.

I wanted to contribute to my community and earn my place in this country.

While working at the church, I kept practicing my English (taking care to double- and triple-check certain words with the people at church) and building a reputation as a hardworking young man. Through some church connections, I was soon offered a job answering phones for the parts department of a local car dealership. I was working so hard, trying to keep pace and do things right, but my English wasn't quite up to par, so I kept pulling the wrong parts. Honest mistakes, but they happened often enough that I felt horrible about it. But my manager and the dealership's owner were patient with me, and that meant so much. I also remember it was the most I'd ever been paid in my life. I was beyond amazed when I got my first paycheck from the dealership. I felt like I'd struck gold!

But eventually, the mistakes piled up, and management pulled me aside. I was a nervous wreck, thinking these guys were going to give me the ax, but instead they asked if I wanted to be a mechanic instead. They asked if I knew anything about European cars, and I enthusiastically said, "Yes, of course!" I was from Europe, after all, albeit the eastern side, and the fact that I barely knew the first thing about cars was irrelevant. I had a strong work ethic, and I was a quick learner.

I ended up interviewing to be a mechanic at a garage that worked on Porsches, Audis, Saabs—all kinds of beautiful European cars. The man I interviewed with was named Tim Presley, and to this day I am convinced he was a relation to the King of Rock and Roll himself. He told me I'd be speaking to each individual brand shop foreman to determine which cars I'd work on exclusively. Some guy named Daryl came in to interview me first. Daryl was a representative for Porsche, very short and stocky. He was quickly frustrated by my lack of English language comprehension and left. The next guy came in a few minutes later. He was affiliated with one of the local motorcycle clubs and must have been seven feet tall! I didn't even catch his name at first, but I knew he worked for Saab. After a short conversation, he asked me if I wanted to work on Saabs; I said yes, with zero hesitation. He mentioned something about how he could definitely use a helper, or slave, as he typically referred to me.

He took me under his wing and taught me everything I needed to know about cars, step by step. His name, I eventually learned, was James Moore. Jim was a party guy, a motorcycle guy, and an all-around wild character, but he was an exceptional mechanic. I swear, he could tell what was wrong with a car just by looking at it. Sometimes he'd get too drunk and crawl under a car and tell me to make random noises around the hood to make it look like we were working and if someone came in to kick him awake.

One night, a few months after I started at the garage, Jim invited me over for a barbeque. I was excited to experience another American "first," having heard stories of Fourth of July parties and casual summer barbeques over the years. I got to Jim's house, a bungalow in a quiet neighborhood in Memphis, and was immediately stunned by the size of the steaks I saw on the grill. These things were massive, literally the biggest cuts of meat I'd ever seen, and there were *three* of them! I asked Jim who all was coming to eat these things, and he said it was just us and another guy from the garage. I couldn't believe it. I was so used to having the tiniest portions of meat in Poland—sausage sandwiches that were mostly bread were never far from my mind—the idea of having all that meat to myself was incredible. One steak was bigger than all the meat I was allowed to buy with ration cards meant to supply food for an entire month in Poland.

At one point during the evening, Jim asked to see some of my karate moves. I was more than happy to put on a little demo for my cool new American friend and, thinking he had concrete walls like we did in Poland, landed a solid punch against his living room wall. Turns out American builders used drywall instead of concrete, and I put my fist right through Jim's wall. I was mortified, but Jim just thought it was hilarious and told me not to worry about it.

Part of my role at the garage was to learn the Saab technical manuals inside and out. However, this was a huge challenge as they were all in English and I was still new to the language. I asked Jim if he could read them aloud for me to help connect the spoken word with the written word to help me understand quicker. I thought this was a great idea; Jim was not impressed with my idea at all. For as tough a guy as he was, his reading skills were not that strong. He eventually agreed, but told me that if I ever told anyone, he would kill me. We would spend hours sitting at the kitchen table eating these juicy American steaks and drinking American beer while Jim labored over the reading of manuals. It was torturous for him, but he did it. He was definitely a better motorcycle rider than book reader. I will be forever grateful to him for reading these manuals and allowing me to record them. I would listen to these recordings for hours and hours at home, focused on trying to match the words on paper with the words I was listening to. Not only did this help me with my job, but it also greatly improved my English, not to mention added some color to my language skills ("shit," "fuck," "goddamn").

While I would eventually go on to work at a Mercedes garage, Jim and I stayed good friends.

These were all huge stepping-stones for me as I continued to acclimate to life in America. As time passed, I came to understand that life in this country wasn't just about working hard day in and day out but also about building friendships and communities with the people around you and helping others. The more people I met and welcomed into my life, the happier I became, and I regularly had to pause and count my blessings that I had been given a chance to do any of it.

I became happier every time I met someone new, and my life became bigger as a result. Shortly after I started my new job with Mercedes, I went on a date with a girl who said she had recently gone skydiving and loved it. I thought it was a crazy idea—who would want to jump out of a perfectly good airplane!—but figured hey, why not. I almost felt obliged to take advantage of every opportunity put in front of me; otherwise, I would be wasting my shot at being an American and enjoying everything this country had to offer.

I went to a skydiving drop zone a couple of weeks later. I remember walking right up to the instructor and asking if I could jump first thing with my own parachute. The instructor was a little surprised, since I was a novice, but said I could start with a tandem jump (jumping with a more experienced person, a certified instructor). I immediately agreed—whatever got me in the air!

The feeling was incredible. Even standing in the door of the plane, waiting to jump, was the most exhilarated I'd ever felt. And then when my hands released their grip on the door and my feet left the floor of the plane, for a moment I thought I was literally flying. I was hooked.

As soon as I landed at the drop zone, I was so amped up I asked the instructor if I could do a tandem jump again. Each time I went up and came down was as good as the first, if not better, because as I became accustomed to the sensations, I was able to do things like look around, enjoy the view from thousands of feet up, and really feel the wind pushing my face back.

After my second tandem jump, I went up to the instructor and asked how I could qualify to jump solo. Regie, my instructor, told me that the process of learning how to skydive through AFF (Accelerated Free Fall) takes anywhere from a week to four weeks. It includes seven jumps (levels) with progressively more difficult tasks that must be successfully performed. I was excited! My course started on Thursday; by Saturday I graduated from AFF and was jumping on my own with a borrowed parachute. I became addicted to skydiving.

Eventually I became so proficient, I figured I might as well try to make some extra money skydiving, so I decided to become a jumpmaster. I attended the AFF jumpmaster course in Tulsa, Oklahoma. It was grueling, but also very fun. During the training, students were paired up with each other and learned about all aspects of skydiving on a totally different, more intense level, which would prepare us for the role of instructor/jumpmaster. Later we had to prepare our lessons and teach them to the fellow skydiver we were paired up with. The evaluating instructors would be seated at the tables to carefully observe our lessons. Our lessons had to be perfect. If you omitted anything from the teaching curriculum or didn't emphasize certain points of skydiving, the evaluating instructor who was observing would remember it for the real skydive, and when pretending to be a student during the actual evaluation jump for each AFF level, the evaluator would deliberately make the mistake based on what you omitted or missed in your lesson.

Once again, my lack of pronunciation skills with the English language didn't help me. We had an agreement between students that when the student who was teaching a lesson asked a question, the other person acting as the student would always answer it correctly, so we would not have to reteach that aspect of skydiving. At one point, I was reviewing the decision-making process for if a student had a malfunction of the main parachute. In case of a main parachute malfunction, by the two-thousand-foot decision-making altitude a student had to decide whether to cut away the malfunctioning main parachute and open the reserve, or whether he would just ride the main canopy to the ground.

We referred to this altitude as the "hard deck." During the review, I asked a standard jump preparation question: "What is your hard deck?"

Instead of the expected, correct answer: two thousand feet, decision-making altitude...I got a weird look and a question from my evaluation partner (aka the student): "What do you mean?"

I repeated, "You know, what is your hard deck?"

His response was, "I can't tell you that."

Now, I was totally mad. Was he trying to trip me up and make sure I failed the course? I didn't understand what the hell had happened to this guy, so I tried a different angle.

"Tell me about your two-thousand-foot hard deck."

I was totally stressed out, and as I looked around to where the USPA commission and instructors were sitting, they were no longer sitting but were rolling with laughter on the ground.

When the guy finally answered that he doesn't have a two-thousand-foot hard dick, I finally got it! It was my pronunciation. I was pronouncing the word "deck" as "dick." I became known around neighboring drop zones as "Geronimo with a two-thousand-foot hard dick." The skydiving nickname my colleagues had given to me was Geronimo, which came from my last name Dzieran, pronounced similar to the Geron in Geronimo.

I became an accelerated freefall jumpmaster in 1988. Besides being a part of the resistance movement in Poland, it was my proudest achievement in life up to that point.

My American life was shaping up nicely. Now thirty years old, I had a long-term girlfriend, a community of friends and neighbors, and was making some decent money between my work as a mechanic and as a jumpmaster teaching skydiving classes to curious Tennesseans. Things were going well for me, and I regularly called my mother back in Poland to give her updates about my life. At that point, the country was still trapped in the clutches of Communism behind the Iron Curtain, but it was obviously on its last legs. I don't know if telling her about America helped or hurt her, but I think it gave her comfort to know that one of her children had made it out before the regime collapsed. Because no one knew what would happen then.

In the meantime, I committed myself to one other course of study: becoming a United States citizen. I encourage you to give the US naturalization test a look if you never have, because even in 1991 when I took it, it was hard. I spent months studying for it, practicing my English language skills with my girlfriend, our friends, and my coworkers. I read countless books on American history and read the newspapers constantly. There was so much information to learn and memorize, but I knew it was for a good reason.

While I was studying and preparing for the naturalization test, I watched and read the news as the Persian Gulf War broke out. I had been so focused on learning American history and current events, I didn't have much sense of who Saddam Hussein was or where Iraq even was on a map. But I knew if it was a question between serving or not serving, there was only one answer I could give.

I became a United States citizen in May 1991, and that immediately became the proudest moment of my life. My family back in Poland was thrilled for me, as were all my friends in America. It was like I'd won the lottery twice! I couldn't believe it. But I'd worked hard for it and succeeded, and I knew now was the time to make good on my decision to fight for the country that had embraced me so fully, even though I had no clue what we were fighting about. I felt it was my moral obligation to support my new country in any way that I could. I wasn't rich enough to create new jobs for my fellow less fortunate American friends, but I could fight for them and for my new adopted country—the people and the country that gave me freedom.

A few days after gaining citizenship, some friends came over to celebrate with me. They didn't expect to walk in on me packing my bags, let alone to hear me telling them that I would be leaving soon "to war."

They were shocked. "Why would you do that?"

"Because I'm an American!"

"How did you sign up?"

"I filled out the paperwork and sent it to them."

In the post office, I had found a Selective Service registration card for the draft. I proudly filled it out, sent it off, and went home to pack my stuff. I was expecting to get a call from the military any time. America was at war, and I was ready to serve. The answer came the next month: Thank you but your age is out for range for Selective Service registration. The Selective Service card is not a contract, as I thought it had been. It is just a mandatory registration tool, and all young American men between the ages of eighteen and twenty-six are required to register and provide their information to the government in case Congress ever implements another draft. If American men between the ages of eighteen and twenty-six are convicted of failing to register as required, they can face up to five years in prison and a fine of up to $250,000.

I found out that thirty-one was a bit old for the Selective Service registration, and that me just sending in paperwork wasn't going to result in anything. I wanted to serve my new country—this big, beautiful place that had already given me so much. I was a free man. I had never had that before. I explained to my friends that when it came to my decision to join the military, *I* wanted to serve because I wanted to do it, not because someone was forcing me or trying to convince me to join. That seemed to satisfy their curiosity, but they still couldn't wrap their heads around the fact that I wanted to go fight somewhere else when I'd just gotten the golden ticket to the easy life. How could I explain to them that that was exactly why I wanted to go fight? It was much more than an expression of gratitude; I felt it was my moral obligation to give back to this country and the people who had given me freedom.

The only real input I got on my plans was from a friend and fellow skydiver who told me to go to the Army recruitment office and explain my situation to them. He said that if I talked to a person, I'd have a better chance of getting in. So, I put together all the necessary paperwork and did just that. I asked my questions and was given the necessary information from the recruiter. After a couple of hours in his office, I was all but officially signed on with the enlistment process and the Army recruiting office started the paperwork with the recruitment process. I was ecstatic—I could now contribute to this great country.

Around this same time, the Navy SEALs jump team (Leap Frogs) happened to come to our drop zone for a few days. They were doing a demonstration jump in Memphis, Tennessee. At that time, I didn't know what the SEALs were. A few guys from our drop zone and I got to do a series of jumps with them, which were all perfect. I told them about my plans to join the military and my talks with the Army recruiters. I was quickly instructed to go and talk to the Navy recruiter and ask about the Navy SEALs.

Happily, but feeling a little awkward for going behind the Army's back so soon after talking to them, I went to the Navy office and told them I was very interested in joining the Navy SEALs. First thing, the recruiter told me, was to go take my paperwork back from the Army. It was the first hurdle—I didn't feel comfortable doing that. But I did.

Then came the next hurdle: at thirty-one I was considered too old to be folded directly into SEAL training. Besides, I had to complete basic training and then A School first, and then hopefully get an age waiver and qualify for

Navy SEAL training. The Navy recruiter assured me that if I only signed the contract, the Navy would make a SEAL out of me for sure! Fine, I thought—at least I was starting the process. I told the recruiter that all sounded good. By that time, most of my paperwork was finished (mostly by the Army recruiter) and I was ready to enlist. As for my job in the Navy, I chose to be a parachute rigger, as I thought it would be the closest thing to skydiving that I could get. The Navy recruiter told me that with all my paperwork completed, the next round of boot camp with the right timing for parachute rigging school started the following week, so there was no time to waste!

It was a rush. All the things I thought I'd have weeks to take care of I had to accomplish in less than a week. As soon as I left the recruiter's office, I ran to the nearest pay phone and called my girlfriend to tell her the news. Of course, she was not thrilled! I still remember her big "WHAAAT?" And then I told her that we needed to get married before I left. She hesitated at first and then said, "Okay." We went and bought each other a couple of small rings, marched over to city hall, and found a judge who'd marry us.

The following Thursday, I was sworn into the U.S. Navy Delayed Entry Program.

That Saturday, I left for boot camp.

★ CHAPTER TWELVE ★

NAVAL JOURNEY

JOINING THE NAVY WAS DISORIENTING and very lonely at first. There I was at thirty-one—considered "old" by enlisted military standards—having built a whole new life for myself in America. I felt like I was starting all over again.

But I was undeterred. I flew to the Great Lakes Naval Training Center near Chicago, Illinois, with a handful of other recruits. When we landed there, Navy buses picked us up from the airport and brought us to the naval station near the south side of Lake Michigan where we'd undergo basic training. We didn't pull into the training facility until late that night, and then it was a huge switch, like we'd walked onto a film set. I stumbled off the bus with all the younger guys I'd traveled with and immediately people were on us, screaming at us, telling us to stand here, put our stuff over there, look down, look up, say *yes, sir* or *no, sir* like this. A couple of young guys ran back to the bus and refused to leave. They wanted to go home.

It was dark and loud and there were lights flashing in our eyes while big, grown men screamed in our faces. For a brief moment amid the chaos I wondered, *What have I gotten myself into?* But my next thought brought me back to reality: I had chosen to do this.

And in any case, after a while I got used to the noise and the people, never having quiet or time to be alone. I'm amazed how humans can adapt so quickly to new circumstances. Once the instructors were satisfied that I could still do push-ups and sit-ups and run, I started taking classes on all kinds of subjects. Navy history, American history, math, science, engineering…I was fascinated by it all and so excited to learn even more about my new home country. Among other things, the Navy taught me that in America, we are all the same color—red, white, and blue.

One unfortunate side effect of getting older, of course, is that your body can do disruptive (and often painful) things at very inconvenient times. In my case, I got a kidney stone while at boot camp.

I had no idea it was a kidney stone at the time. All I knew was that one moment I was in my bunk trying to get a few precious minutes of sleep, and the next moment I was on the floor sweating huge puddles of salty water, in the worst, most agonizing pain of my life. I thought someone had stabbed me in the kidney, and having taken a lot of beatings there, I more or less knew the feeling. My fellow recruits called for help, and I was taken to the Navy emergency room, where I was given some strong drugs to help pass the time and eventually the kidney stone.

Before boot camp, I had taken and passed my Armed Services Vocational Aptitude Battery (ASVAB) test with flying colors, which meant I was on track to graduate from basic training and be eligible for SEAL training. But after the kidney stone incident, that track hit a snag. The Navy was now concerned about my health history, and following

Navy protocols, they deferred me from applying to SEAL training for a year. They also recommended to roll me back to the next boot camp class. I was disappointed, to say the least, and it was annoying to have gone through all that education and training only to have to start back at square one in a year. However, I was determined to stay and was able to convince the medical staff to let me continue with my current boot camp class. At the end of the day, my ultimate goal was to serve my country in the best capacity I could.

I graduated from boot camp as the number one recruit with a Military Excellence Award.

My next and last stop before I finally went to begin SEAL training was Navy A School, where basic training graduates get technical training in their chosen military occupational specialty (NEC) field. Aircrew Survival Equipmentman was the Navy job I applied for, and I would travel to Millington, Tennessee, for training. After all of my training and work experience, this part of my Navy experience was almost easy. It was very technical, and attention to detail was paramount. Parachute riggers were responsible for maintaining the ejection seat parachutes, as well as the pilots' and crew's survival equipment. We literally held their lives in our hands.

While in Millington, I visited a Navy SEAL motivator on base. I asked to take the initial SEAL entry test, and I passed it. Then I told him the situation with my kidney stone. He thought for a minute and told me to bring my medical record to his office. Sure—I ran to the clinic on base, with his chit/request for my medical record, and I was back with it in an hour. The record of my kidney stone was on the first page. The Navy SEAL motivator, Lester, told me to wait outside his office. I could hear a loud rip and was called back into the office. He looked at me with concern and said that he was not able to find any record of my kidney stone, anywhere. He asked me if I could point it out for him. As we trudged through my medical record, I could not find it either. Then looking carefully at me, he asked me if I was sure that I ever had a kidney stone. At that point I was already 100 percent convinced that I didn't.

CHAPTER THIRTEEN

SEAL TIME, NOW

I HAD NO IDEA WHAT I was in for.

Originally, I was under the impression that SEAL trainees basically disappeared into a black box for months on end, but that wasn't the case at all. While there wasn't much free time while in BUD/S (Basic Underwater Demolition/SEAL) training, the younger guys in my class often went out drinking after training days, but being the old guy of the group, I was always so exhausted after training that most of the time I would stay behind on base and try to get as much sleep as I could. It was on the rare occasion that I would go out with my fellow students for a drink.

The process of becoming a SEAL is BUD/S training, which are six of the most physically exhausting months of anyone's life. Men have died, or nearly died, during BUD/S training—it's that intense. I wasn't deterred by that fact, but I definitely felt the intensity, crawling into bed completely wiped at the end of every day. I still don't know where those younger guys found the strength to go and party after the day was over.

My attitude was a bit different than others' when it came to BUD/S training. I once overheard some of the guys talking about "trying" this and "attempting" that, wanting to be "the best" or "the strongest," that kind of stuff. Posturing. When the question came around to me, I responded with the truth: "I'm not here to 'try' to do anything. I'm here to become a Navy SEAL and serve my country. I am not here to try; I am here to become one."

While my age didn't hold me back from keeping up with, if not outright outpacing, the younger guys in physical training, it showed itself in other ways. As I said, I didn't party as much as the other guys, and I didn't drink. I had years and experience on many of my classmates. None of the other guys had grown up under Communist oppression either, so they didn't know how lucky they'd had it growing up in America.

During the first phase of training, the most physical part of the training, instructors were motivated to weed out the guys who weren't capable of becoming or ready to be SEALs. These instructors were very effective—a number of guys in my class folded during the first phase—but I was never too bothered by it. I had taken more than my share of beatings and harassment over the years in Poland, after all; I knew these instructors weren't going to kill me, so what did I have to worry about? It didn't take long before they started skipping over me to yell at other guys since they knew I wasn't affected by the verbal abuse.

My biggest issue was that I wasn't the strongest swimmer. The best I could do was a sidestroke, and only on one side. Swimming with a diving mask on was torture, too—I legitimately thought I was going to pass out and drown at one point. I remember seeing black spots swimming across my vision because I was trying to breathe through my nose, which was stopped up by the mask I was wearing. I ended up swallowing so much water I came out with a huge, distended stomach. But I kept swimming, knowing that if I passed out or started drowning, the instructor and the other guys would fish me out and resuscitate me.

As I got better with time, my sidestroke apparently made an impression. When the next class of SEAL trainees came in behind mine, I was chosen to show the new guys how to do it. I was very proud of myself for that.

During First Phase, which is the seven-week-long period following three weeks of BUD/S orientation, my classmates and I were told to go on a mud run. It was the week before the infamous Hell Week, which was how the Navy in a large part determined if someone was cut out for the SEAL program, and it was then that I got a nasty cut on my leg. I was fine at first, finishing the mud run with flying colors, but by the weekend, the whole limb was so swollen I couldn't take my pants off. I had to cut the one pant leg off at mid-thigh and once again hobbled over to the medical unit.

Medics poked around the wound, diagnosed it as MRSA, and said they'd clean it and bandage me up but that I'd probably have to be rolled over into the next class as a result. I said no way, so they told me to go on a run. It was highly discouraged to see a doctor and miss any training. You should be able to handle whatever pain you were in, so long as it didn't result in death or permanent injury. So, minutes after the medics cut my leg open and drained my wound, I went outside and ran a mile on it. I managed, but it was a struggle. Even though I was able to run, I was not allowed to continue and was rolled back to class 185. I had to start training again, from the very beginning.

And then, just like that, it was Hell Week.

The first night, we were placed in barracks and told to wait for "Hell" to break out. Guys were peeking through the windows, trying to see if someone was outside in the dark. We waited for what felt like hours, but it could have been minutes—there was no real way of knowing. Once they'd closed the door behind us, time was irrelevant. All that mattered was what was happening in the moment.

And when Hell Week started, it really started—suddenly, M-60 guns began firing blank rounds all at once, filling the air with noise, and then we were chased out of the barracks, sprayed down with freezing cold water out of strong hoses, then ordered to do a hundred jumping jacks, push-ups, and sit-ups each. A few of us, including myself, burst out laughing at the absurdity of the situation.

A couple of hours later, we weren't laughing anymore.

If we didn't run fast enough, we had to walk into the ocean arm in arm and lie down in the surf until our lips turned blue. Afterward, we'd sit freezing in the sand and the instructors would walk up and down the line, screaming, "Who's gonna quit? Who's gonna ring that bell, huh? We're not going anywhere until someone gets up and rings that bell." It was a tactic on their part, to see who was liable to break under pressure and sheer cold. There was always a guy or two who would use the instructors' taunts as an excuse to quit, claiming he was doing it for the class as he stood up and walked over to the bell—a single brass bell rigged to some rope and a two-by-four. The three stark rings of the brass bell signaled that he had reached his own personal limits; he gave up and could take no more. In reality it was not a choice made for the team, but an individual decision to "volunteer out" of SEAL training. The bell was still vibrating as we headed back to the sand for more surf torture; that guy saved no one but himself.

A large portion of guys who drop out of BUD/S training do so during Hell Week, usually for one of two reasons: injury or cold. Cold is tough to deal with, but some injuries you can push through, like I did.

Every night during Hell Week, the entire class had to undergo physical exams. The reason for this—besides the fact that Hell Week is brutal on the body—is that after a few days of it, your brain is so gone on adrenaline, exhaustion, stress, and being freezing cold all the time that you might not realize if you've been injured. Some guys would keep training on broken legs, broken arms, fractured hips, sprained ankles, concussions, open sores, and all kinds of injuries because they couldn't feel it. Some who had been training on severe injuries had to leave BUD/S during these inspections, even if they didn't want to, simply because their body was too badly injured to continue training without risking disability or death.

The SEAL instructors must have had a great time observing us during those seemingly crazy Hell Week exercises. One particularly memorable event was the night they built a huge bonfire on the beach and told us to strip down and warm up. We were thrilled, dumping our wet, freezing clothes in a pile on the beach and standing naked in front of the fire under the dark, clear sky. Five minutes later, they told us to get dressed again—we had to put on the cold wet clothes that were now full of sand. Miserable. Some guys dropped out right then and there.

Past day four of Hell Week, time becomes a blur. It doesn't feel like a memory now, more like a really intense dream I once had. I remember at one point, we were paddling out on the water and my swim buddy, Rich, was on my right. (Every trainee is assigned a "swim buddy" at the beginning of BUD/S, and that person is literally no less than three feet from your side 24/7.) When I looked to my left, I saw a huge glass tower coming out of the ocean. I tried reaching out to touch it and a guy behind me shouted, "What are you doing? Focus!"

"Can't you see the glass tower?" I said, awestruck.

"What glass tower?"

"This one here!"

"Oh, I see it!" he finally said.

And just like that, we were collectively hallucinating.

I wasn't the only one. Throughout the week guys would hallucinate all kinds of things. One trainee thought he saw a spotlight and ran into the ocean to chase it; instructors had to run in after him and bring him back on land.

Much like prison, Hell Week is full of pain and discomforts both big and small. When we weren't lying down in the sand being half drowned by the incoming surf or doing mud runs, we were lifting, hauling, and throwing heavy things up and down the beach until we thought our arms would fall off. Even the strongest guys felt like weaklings after days of constant strain and abuse. We even had to run to chow with inflatable boats balanced on our heads. Some guys lost the hair on top of their heads from the bottoms of the boats chafing against them for so long. No matter what, the instructors made sure that every last one of us was physically exhausted.

When Hell Week was almost over, my feet had swollen from size ten to size thirteen. But we made it! Between the relief of getting to the end of it all and the joy of finally getting to lie in a bed in dry clothes, I passed out as soon as my head hit the pillow. After Hell Week, we were restricted to barracks for twenty-four hours to make sure that everybody was okay and no injuries showed up. Also, not sleeping for four to five days negatively affects some students' judgment. After the mandatory twenty-four-hour lockdown, when the younger guys went out drinking to celebrate, I slept.

Reaching the end of Hell Week is like being reborn. There's really no better way to describe the feeling. I was *invincible*. But while my thoughts went one way, my body went another, and I could barely get out of bed the next day. When I finally did, I noticed that my boots had basically disintegrated, and my feet were even worse. I eventually got up to take a shower and most of the skin came right off my feet. That was somewhat painful to look at.

But I'd done what I'd set out to do: I was through Hell Week.

The remaining three weeks of First Phase training were much gentler on our bodies but still grueling. That period involved more technical classroom stuff and doing Navy-specific tasks like hydrography, the science of surveying and charting bodies of water. We went on timed runs and spent a good chunk of time in the pool being tested on various skills. Eventually class 185 moved to the second phase of training: diving. A lot of people assume most guys who fall out of SEAL training do so during Hell Week, but in fact, most of them (at least in my class) fell out during pool competency training. This was because it was basically a pass/fail class: if you failed the training twice, you could take it again the next day, but if you failed again, your SEAL training was pretty much over unless the command decided to roll you over to the next class.

Second Phase was so technical, so precise, so procedure-driven that any wrong thing was an almost instant failure. The pressure was way more psychological than physical in Second Phase, although the physical factor was still very real. This was the seven-week period when trainees spent hours in a pool together every day, studying dive physics and learning how to swim, breathe, dive, and function in the water like a SEAL. The further into the phase we got, the harder the exercises became, until we had progressed from timed swims to combat SCUBA. Like other training phases, we were working toward timed goals as well as examinations, where we'd be tested on our skills, competency, and general comfort in the water.

I failed my dive physics exam, and as a punishment, all of us who failed had to face the "Wheel of Misfortune." Just like the original Wheel of Fortune, we had to spin the wheel and win our "prizes," but the prizes were not money or goods, they were wet and sandy push-ups, sit-ups, or jumping jacks. When you spun the wheel and the arrow stopped on the designated field, you had to perform the "won" exercise. After a few hours, we were allowed to go back to the barracks and study for the retake of dive physics. A few other guys and I stayed up late to study. We were all stressing out big-time, constantly sweating and pacing the room. We were able to retake the test and pass, but after that, I was determined to pass every test the first time.

Unfortunately, I failed my first pool competency test too. I did not complete the required procedure correctly, but I passed it on the second try.

After seven weeks in the water, it was time for Third Phase: Land Warfare.

Third Phase covered everything the previous phases had not: things like basic weapons training, land navigation, marksmanship, and tactics. Made up of both day and night exercises, Third Phase started off with a lot of classroom time learning stuff like how to read a compass or a map before we started applying what we were learning to exercises out in the field. This was around the time things started to feel more real for those of us who were still in the class—we could see the light at the end of the tunnel, so to speak.

BUD/S training proved I was capable of a lot of things, but it also revealed a lot of ways in which I wasn't as strong as I thought. I was never a fast runner, but I could run for miles when going slow on long distances, for example, and Third Phase highlighted this fact for me. At one point during this phase, we had to do a ruck march under the scorching California sun, and I hadn't been drinking nearly enough water. After the ruck, I panicked to see that I was pissing blood. The medic told me not to worry about it and to just keep drinking water, but that was the moment when I realized my body wasn't as young as I felt and was starting to break down with age. After that incident, I couldn't recover from dehydration nearly as fast as I could when I was younger, and I had to take that into account whenever I went out in the field.

We also got to spend a few days up on Mount Laguna as part of our land navigation training during this phase. Up on the mountain, we did things like compass training, radio usage, communications, living rough, living at altitude, and all kinds of stuff.

Land navigation was one of the more enjoyable parts of BUD/S training for me. It consisted of each of us being given coordinates to a location, a map, a compass, and not much else. During the day it was okay since we had sunlight to see and navigate by, but at night things got treacherous. At one point while trying to find my way in the dark, I slipped off a short cliff and broke my flashlight and lost my map. I didn't panic—I just turned around 180 degrees, going by the compass, and returned to the starting camp. It only took me about an hour, but I worried the whole way that I was going to get my shit chewed out for failing the night exercise. But when I explained the situation to the instructors, they seemed to be somewhat impressed by me finding my way back to camp without the map and didn't punish me too much. They let me try again the next night. Although I wasn't overly proud of losing my map and breaking my flashlight, they ended up using me as an example for the class on how to deal with such adversity.

While in the camp on Mount Laguna, every hour, one guy had to be on watch and in communication with other groups around and down the mountain. One guy fell asleep on watch one night; as punishment, he had to douse his head with cold water once an hour every hour. I felt bad for him and gave him my gloves, which he'd lost somewhere farther down the mountain during our ruck to camp. When we got back to the base on Coronado, he gave me my gloves back and dropped out. I never saw him again.

From the outside, this training seems absurd, and it is brutal, but everything that happens during SEAL training is taken from a carefully curated and calculated training guide that is updated and improved upon year after year (although plenty of exercises, like carrying a boat on your head, stick around). There are no random exercises, and if it's not in the manual, it's not part of the training. Unlike the popular belief that some exercises are just arbitrarily made up and crazy, in SEAL training, there is no randomness or haphazard foolishness. Everything goes by the book and manuals. The training is dangerous as it is; there is no place for craziness. There are many safety measures implemented to protect students. Most of it is invisible to trainees. They don't know about it, and this is one of the ways to induce extra stress on students so they can be graded on how they perform under duress.

But the ordeal wasn't over yet. Next was five weeks on San Clemente Island where, as the saying goes, "No one can hear you scream." We spent a month on this island off the coast of California, and it was where we got to apply a lot of the lessons we'd learned in training: land warfare, fire and maneuver, land navigation, radio communications, and more. We were always cold, always wet, always awake, and often hungry. My appetite went through the roof. That light at the end of the tunnel seemed to get a little bit smaller every day, but we really started to feel like SEALs, operating as a unit, learning to rely on each other, and applying the skills we'd learned.

Naturally, the instructors kept up the "torture." Before each meal there was a ritual: if you wanted to eat inside you had to do eleven pull-ups with your full kit on (which could weigh enough to prevent some of us from doing the required perfect pull-ups). If you didn't do those pull-ups correctly, in lieu of another attempt you were told to sprint down to the ocean, get wet, and sprint back up the hill with great motivation. You were given a set time to accomplish it. If you didn't make the instructor's time, you had to do it again. When the instructor was done with you, only then were you allowed to eat, and you had to stay outside for the failed pull-ups.

The instructors had a blast with us, but we also had a good time. We were learning new skills and getting proficient at them, renewing our motivation. Those five weeks were physically worse than Hell Week, in my opinion. For me, it felt like Hell Week on steroids. I think it was because it incorporated all the worst parts of the previous phases, and we were doing it having already gone through those phases. We went from exhausted, beaten, and in pain to worse.

One night on San Clemente, a classmate got caught trying to dry his clothes in a dryer. His punishment was a full night of running circles around the barracks, jumping in a freezing water tank filled with ice, and screaming "I'll never dry my clothes again!" every ten laps. He managed, but it was hard to watch, and even harder to keep from laughing out loud.

The whole time I was training to become a SEAL, I was still working very hard to improve my English skills. By the time I got to San Clemente, my English was better than ever, but it was still pretty rough. I regularly had to translate what I was trying to say in English to Polish and back into English again just to communicate with people. During a land warfare phase on San Clemente Island, we were training with live ammunition. We had to communicate while shooting and moving, passing the verbal commands with our team. At times I didn't yell loud enough and was getting awarded extra motivational exercises (motivational push-ups, sit-ups, etc.). The instructors were very observant, and no infraction went unpunished. During live-fire exercises, I was concentrating on the firing and maneuvering with my element so much that I did not pass commands loud enough once again. Another student and I were given two-by-four planks of wood and were told to continue the exercise with our planks instead of a rifle. We were instructed to imitate the sound and yell "Pow, Pow, Pow" loud enough to drown the sound of our fellow students firing their real rifles. Thirty minutes later I had a huge headache from screaming so insanely loud while the instructors kept yelling at me to scream even louder. I almost lost my voice the next day. I knew my ability to speak English would matter downrange, so I made it a point to learn and practice more until I'd mastered the language. Much like parachute rigging, communication was a matter of life and death in combat, and I was going to master it.

I understood the point of the intense training and selection: to acquire and internalize the skills and knowledge necessary to accomplish the mission and keep you and your fellow SEALs alive.

★ CHAPTER FOURTEEN ★

WELCOME TO THE TEAMS

AT THAT TIME, ONCE YOU completed BUD/S training, you went to jump school. After that, you would report to your first assigned SEAL Team, where you would complete STT (SEAL Tactical Training, what is now SEAL Qualification Training or SQT) and then be assigned to a SEAL platoon. You still had not earned your Trident and were on probation. It was seldom, but some did not make it through probationary period and were sent away to the regular fleet without ever earning the coveted SEAL Trident. If your assigned SEAL platoon said you passed muster, you would get your Trident and become a Navy SEAL. It is different nowadays. Today, the SEAL Trident is awarded after successful graduation from SQT.

Jump school was out of Fort Benning in Georgia. It was January or February, so the weather was not too bad. We had already learned how to deal with the cold pretty well. The Army had a nice facility and nice grounds; the place was like Disneyland to some of us. Not only that, but we'd out-PT the Army guys left and right, which was always fun.

And when it came time to do jumps, I was so excited to be doing them at Fort Benning—the birthplace of the United States Airborne and the concept of parachute infantry. The training and preparations for the first jump were a lot of fun, too. The facility in Fort Benning is well equipped and organized to safely push thousands of soldiers through the training. The towers we had to jump from attached to the harness and the zip lines reminded me of amusement parks in Poland that I could not afford to play in. I definitely abused that nostalgia, going multiple times to jump, slide, and play. It was like an amusement park for me, and I loved every second of it.

Given my education and training as a civilian AFF jumpmaster, this jump school training was easy. There was one key difference between what I'd learned as a civilian jumpmaster and actual military parachute jumps: landing with the round military parachutes required the use of PLFs (Parachute Landing Falls). In civilian skydiving, we jumped with RAM-AIR square parachutes and PLFs were seldom necessary, if at all; however, when jumping with military round parachutes at a high rate of descent, a PLF is mandatory.

PLFs look like they should be easy. But for some reason, the PLF was the only thing I did in training that scared me. Something about falling to the ground at top speed, and landing and falling over *on purpose* was terrifying to me. The jump was one thing, I loved it; performing a PLF was another, I hated it. In Army airborne training, after you jump, the static line attached to the aircraft pulls your round parachute out for you, and you prepare to land by way of PLF. The PLF is completed in this manner: you put your feet and knees together, touch down on the balls of your feet, and immediately start into a rolling fall along your side—calf, thigh, hip—moving the roll up the side of the back to distribute the force and minimize impact from the high-speed landing.

Every time I went to land during the jumps, instead of performing the required PLF like I was supposed to, I'd land on my feet and stop there. The instructors (aka Black Hats as they were called for the black ball caps they wore) hated that, and when they caught me doing it, they yelled at me to do the PLF or I would not be allowed on the next jump. I'd be there standing upright in the process of rolling my parachute, but an order is an order—I had to drop my parachute and ever so gently ease myself to the ground imitating the PLF. I just rolled to the ground to satisfy my instructors and then continued to roll my chute into a bag. I never managed to jump and perform the PLF the way I was supposed to. I always preferred to make stand-up landings while jumping the MC-1B round parachutes.

☆ ☆ ☆

Being assigned to my first SEAL Team was unlike anything I'd ever experienced before.

At that point in the training process, you are technically a part of your assigned Team, able to take on basic duties and train, but you're not a SEAL yet. No, when you first join a SEAL Team you're known as an "FNG," or "Fucking New Guy." That name sticks until you fall out or complete one overseas deployment. Don't be fooled: even at this stage nothing guarantees that you will succeed in becoming a SEAL. Getting through this phase of SEAL training was extremely high stakes. I knew guys who fell out at this stage.

When I checked in to my new Team in March 1993, I showed up trying to look my sharpest. I'd pressed my best uniform until it was perfect, had all my papers in hand and ready to present, and I walked smartly right on into SEAL Team Two's quarterdeck.

Like a Fucking New Guy.

I was greeted by the quarterdeck watch, my paperwork was inspected, and I was told to wait in front of Command Master Chief's office. After introducing myself to the CMC, I was instructed to follow one of the SEALs to the back of the compound and complete my initial check-in process.

As soon as I was out of sight of the CMC and walking through the compound, I was stopped by other SEALs, told to jump on the pull-up bars, and keep doing pull-ups until told to dismount the pull-up bars. From there, things got fast and painful. After pull-ups, I was yelled at to lay down and do sit-ups, then push-ups, then I was ushered out of the SEAL Team through the back gate, marched to the starting point of the three-mile run testing route and told to complete the run in the required time. Mind you, I was still wearing my dress blues uniform and perfectly polished shoes. By the time the older SEALs finished with me, my awesome uniform looked like sweats for playing basketball. I did well on this unofficial Physical Readiness Test (PRT), and was left alone to complete the official onboarding process. I was assigned a cage in the locker, issued the initial gear, and proceeded with the paperwork and other formalities. As I found out later, this "unexpected and informal" PRT test was often just a part of the "Welcome FNG to the SEAL Team" routine.

In the evening, I went to the Navy Exchange and purchased a new uniform.

Of course, this was only the beginning of the indoctrination of new guys to the Teams.

The next day, I was told to report to the paraloft (parachute loft) at the back of SEAL Team Two compound. This is where I would work while waiting for the next stage of my training, SEAL Tactical Training (STT).

At this stage, you're learning from the older guys. Veteran SEALs—guys who've already deployed, some four or five times, maybe more—train the new guys as a rule. And training in this case was less physically demanding but a lot more tedious. Our job as FNGs was to do everything the older SEALs told us to do—in addition to the regular technical and tactical training, we had to clean this, pick up that, stand here, run over there.

During one of the qualification jumps at the local drop zone, when the ramp on the C-130 opened and we were ready to jump, one of the old SEALs, Steve, turned to me and yelled, "Hey you FNG! God doesn't have the balls to kill me on this jump! What do you think?" I gasped, made the sign of the cross, thinking *Jesus, are you crazy?* But this guy jumped and wore a big grin on his face the whole way down to the ground.

I was taken off guard by what he'd said, but it stuck with me. I went on to say the same thing to young guys when I became a seasoned, experienced SEAL. And the effect was always the same: "Jesus Christ, Drago, are you a mad man?" The look on the new guys' faces made me laugh.

At that time, it was a SEAL Team Two custom that on every Friday afternoon after work, the guys would gather in the High Bay with a keg of beer. The High Bay was a tall engineering space within the SEAL Team Two compound that stored tools, chains, and various trucks and pullies used to lift heavy equipment.

One Friday, the older guys invited us FNGs to join them for a kegger. As a new guy, I was impressed at what I thought was their genuine interest in team building. We were all looking forward to the end of the day, honestly. I remember thinking, *Oh wow, these older experienced SEALs are inviting us to join them for beers! How awesome!* We felt like the popular kids had just invited us to sit with them at lunch. I quickly learned, however, that we weren't there to build camaraderie or to hang out with the popular kids. We were there for the amusement of the veteran SEALs; this was them giving us an old-school Navy SEAL welcome.

The cool old guys jumped us and bound our feet with rigger's tape. Then they hung us from the High Bay's ceiling with cranes and chain lifts. Of course, there were more than a few punches thrown in throughout to minimize our resistance to their "welcome." We soon found ourselves hanging from the ceiling like big, grumpy bats. Every once in a while, we were lowered down from the ceiling for a swig of beer or another beating or to be laughed at when our faces changed another shade of red. We weren't back on our feet until the "kegger" was over.

While this ritual might be considered hazing by outsiders, it was meant to be a kind of testing ground for the new guys. We had to prove we were tough enough to be trusted in any situation.

Today there are no longer "Kegger Fridays" in the SEAL Teams, and no alcohol is allowed in the compound. Very strict policies regarding alcohol are now in place. "The Ole Welcome to the Teams" has been softened and put under control so the new "welcome procedures" are not mistaken for hazing. There are very strict policies in place regarding any welcome events.

But at that time, it was all "good to go."

We were the FNGs until we completed at least one overseas deployment.

There were other less intense moments from my time working with SEAL Team Two that I can think back on now and laugh. My accent, especially, provided a lot of opportunities for jokes. For example, the first time I stood watch on quarterdeck with another SEAL, I was ordered to put out a call for someone to come to the quarterdeck, which meant my voice got blasted all over the compound.

"Petty Officer Second Class John Smith, please report to the quarterdeck."

It got quiet. Suddenly, from the compound of SEAL Team Two I could hear voices: "What the *fuck* was that?" Out of one door came the master chief; a second door opened, and the commanding officer came out; a third door opened, and the executive officer came out shouting, "What the fuck! Quarterdeck Watch, did you lose your mind?"

"What did you just say?" one officer demanded.

"I called Petty Officer Smith to the quarterdeck, sir."

They looked at each other. "Oh. And you really talk like that? Funny?"

"Yes, sir. This is my accent. I can't change it, but I will work on it harder."

There was a long pause, and then one of them shrugged a little and said, "Okay." And that was that. The older guys made their peace with it, but not without plenty of ribbing afterward.

The issue of my heavy Polish accent and English skills followed me to STT. During this advanced training, it was the same thing—my English wasn't very good, but I was managing it well enough—only now, on top of it, I had to learn tons of new information at a high level, which made things even harder.

During the SEAL Tactical Training, we progressed through different blocks of training, learning different skills—land warfare, land navigation, diving, radio communication and encryption, demolition and explosives, etc.

Eventually, the rest of my STT class and I moved on to the radio communications and encryption block of training where we learned how to use communication and cryptography equipment, encrypt/decrypt coded messages, and so on. I sat through the entire weeklong class, and sitting next to me the whole time was my friend Scott, who was originally from Great Britain. At the end of this block of training, the day before we were supposed to take the final exam required to pass, the instructor walked up to Scott and me as we sat at our desks and asked, "Hey, uh…Do you two have clearance?"

Scott and I looked at each other. "Clearance for what? What is that?"

"Secret clearance. You have to have it to take this training."

I shrugged my shoulders a little bit. "I do not."

The instructor nodded; he looked a little pale. Looking at Scott he asked, "Do you have secret clearance to take this course?"

"No, sir," Scott replied, "I'm not even a U.S. citizen!"

The instructor jumped like he'd been shocked with a cattle prod. "Oh, *shit!*" he said. "You two come out here with me." After we left the classroom, he quietly said, "Everything you learned is extremely sensitive information. You two won't tell *anyone* that you were sitting in this class this past week. *You were never here.*" He told us to come back when we both received the proper clearances, review the materials we'd learned that week, and take the exam. We were never to mention having taken the class to anyone.

We agreed, of course. But it was very strange, watching the other guys take the exam the next day, running around with radios and bent over encryption equipment, communicating with each other. I knew I could have passed that exam, but Scott and I just had to sit quietly on the sidelines and pretend we didn't know anything.

I had to wait five months to receive my secret clearance, but I filled that time with more parachute training, special operation parachute rigging in particular. I finally became very good at it, so I'd say I used the time wisely. Later on, I learned that because of my being a former Polish citizen, my background check had taken longer than average, which is why I didn't have the necessary security clearance to take that course. Which made sense, but I was amazed that no one had noticed the problem until the day before the exam. (Scott had to take a longer detour on his path to become a SEAL—he had to first become a U.S. citizen. He became a citizen a few months later and got his clearance then, right before our first deployment. All of us from the SEAL platoon went to his citizenship ceremony, and he passed his comms/crypto exam afterwards.)

After completion of STT, we were still not SEALs quite yet. We, as new guys, were on the probationary period assigned to a SEAL platoon. After the probationary period and passing the SEAL board made up of chiefs and officers, we were awarded a Navy SEAL Trident.

In the morning muster, in front of the entire SEAL Team Two, we were called up front and center and were presented with the coveted Tridents in the presence of Admiral (today) Joseph Maguire. It was a great milestone in my life. It was a great moment, but it also made me reflect on many things. It was crystallizing in my mind that this could only happen in America, such an exceptional country. Only in America is it possible to come without even knowing the language and carry only a bag of clothes, and still succeed through hard work and determination. As much as I was proud of my SEAL Trident, there was even greater honor that was bestowed on me before. It was American citizenship. The citizenship and American flag encompass the Trident. I was a Trident wearer because I was an American.

The other new SEALs and I headed to the lockers after the ceremony, only to be surrounded by the older guys from SEAL Team Two, whose way of congratulating us was to remove our brand-new Tridents from our uniforms, remove the clasp from the sharp post, and let each guy take a turn punching the pins back into our chests, in a slightly different spot each time.

By the end of the day, I looked like I'd been stuck by a porcupine.

CHAPTER FIFTEEN

THE MISSIONS BEGIN

FIRST DEPLOYMENT
ITALY, 1995–1996

Two months after I'd received my Trident and officially become a SEAL, we deployed to Italy.

Right after arrival, it happened that one of the first things I did was beat up a couple of Air Force guys.

It's not that wild of a story, but here's what happened: A few other SEALs and I were on the dance floor at this little club, and some of the other American servicemen were there and getting rowdy, so I told one of them to stop. That quickly turned into a minor brawl. I ended up getting grounded for it and caught hell from my own platoon, but old habits really do die hard.

In a platoon, you do everything the older guys tell you to do. On top of that, you have your own jobs and responsibilities to stay on top of things. On those rare nights off, we would go out for drinks.

There was one guy on the Team, Bill, who was one of the toughest guys in the platoon. Anytime he walked into a room or bar where we were, we immediately straightened up and told ourselves to get our act together and be on our best behavior. Bill strolled up to us one night and called out, "What's up, meat!" We happily greeted him, buying him drinks and hoping to buddy up to him. He was an experienced SEAL with years of expertise and qualifications; he was smart, but he was a hard-core guy, so we both respected him and feared him a little bit. We figured if we all drank together, he'd loosen up and we'd be free to ask him the questions we would never ask him sober.

The reality was, drinking only made Bill meaner, so instead of joking around and telling us stories about his experiences as a SEAL, he just sat there staring at us. We were on our best behavior after that and made sure to show Bill due deference, but we didn't really offer to buy him drinks anymore. In the end, he taught us a great deal of what we needed to know about the SEAL trade to become successful SEALs. Bill was a good, respected SEAL operator.

Soon after we landed in Italy, we were sent on our mission: to find and, if possible, rescue a downed pilot from behind enemy lines. An American pilot had been forced to eject from his plane, then had to survive a week on his own in hostile territory before he was rescued. SEALs were among those sent in to look for him. At this point, the full realization that it was real now hit me—I was no longer in training. There are so many safety nets in training precisely to make sure that students don't get injured during the training; however, these safeguards are no longer there during missions, and you must rely on your training and your teammates to reduce the chance of injury and ensure mission success.

From the moment I first checked in to SEAL Team Two, it dawned on me that every day we were doing something that could kill us—the training, obstacle courses, parachuting, diving, swimming in the open ocean. I remember during one of the flights over the Adriatic looking for the downed pilot, one of my teammates, Scott, was sitting on the edge of the helicopter's ramp, legs dangling with his head leaning out of the helo. He had a safety belt on him to keep him from falling out, but at one point it slipped off by some freak accident. He was sitting on the edge of the ramp with his safety belt unbuckled, laying behind him. Bill carefully walked back to Scott, grabbed him, and pulled him away from the ramp inside the helo. We were afraid that if we yelled to Scott, he would move and fall off of the ramp. This would be tragic. It was not merely theoretical— we had actually lost a SEAL in a similar manner before.

It was narrow escapes like that that reminded us we weren't in training anymore.

☆ ☆ ☆

When I came back from my first deployment, there was no rest. Being a SEAL is a full-time job; you don't train for months to sit at home and wait for a phone call. SEALs do even more training between missions and deployments to keep ourselves and our skills fresh and honed. Diving, jump training, sniper school—there was always something new to learn or an old skill to improve or expand on.

Usually, after completing an overseas deployment, we could apply for different training programs and various schools. New guys (now former new guys) got to go to these schools to catch up with older SEALs. What school you got depended greatly on your Team's need, but usually you got the school you wanted to go to. After two weeks of post-deployment leave when I returned to the SEAL Team Two compound, I found our guys talking with excitement about their school assignments—sniper School, diving supervisor, jumpmaster, etc. They were curious to hear what school I got. I was assigned to English 101 school on base in Little Creek. As guys would pass me in Navy buses on the street on their way to their respective schools, they would shout at me, "Hey Drago, where are you going?"

I'd hold up my heavy textbook: "I'm going to English class!"

★ CHAPTER SIXTEEN ★

THE MISSIONS CONTINUE

SECOND DEPLOYMENT
GERMANY AND BOSNIA, 1997–1998

One of the best parts about the SEAL Teams is having the ability to move between platoons as needed. Sometimes a guy with particular skills is needed somewhere other than his current location, so he goes. Each SEAL Team has multiple platoons—enough to cover all operational areas around the world, wherever we are needed. (There remains some division between the East Coast and West Coast SEAL Teams, but the same can be said for the civilians who live on either coast, too.)

After finishing my English course, I was assigned to Charlie Platoon at SEAL Team Two, and after many months of work-up we went to Germany. It was a great platoon. Over the course of six months in Germany, we rotated to Bosnia with our sister platoon.

Over the course of my time in the SEAL Teams, I got to meet some really fascinating people. Growing up in

Communist Poland, I certainly had never expected that I would find myself among guys like Chris Stroup, Chief Leif, Lt. B., Lt. F., Barrett, Ron, Magua, John, Steve, Robert, and many other great warriors.

Chris Stroup was the strongest guy I ever met in the SEAL Teams. He was the biggest guy in our platoon, and of course the M-60 gunner. Because of his strength and size, Chris became a fixture and a perpetual M-60 gunner in the SEAL Teams. He was also the one who set us all up with workout routines while we were deployed. He built entire programs for us, from running to weightlifting. And by the end of our sixth-month deployment, each of us weighed over two hundred pounds of pure muscle. The days became almost routine: wake up, work out, eat, work out, train, work out. (SEAL: Sleep, Eat, And Lay around.) Chris was the one who really got us into great physical shape.

But the biggest influence on me in my SEAL career, the guy I always wanted to emulate, was Chief Leif.

Chief Leif was a great leader. Not only was he one of the toughest, he was also dedicated to making us the best SEAL operators there were. I swear, this guy never slept. He was always trying to think of ways to make the platoon harder, better, stronger. His knowledge and expertise were legendary, especially in winter/arctic warfare. He taught us how to ice climb, ski, navigate arctic environments, everything. Nobody else in SEAL Team Two knew as much as Chief Leif—who in his late thirties was also older than most SEALs—about that stuff.

But at the end of the day, Chief Leif was a very quiet guy and kept to himself most of the time. He worked closely with the platoon officer in charge (OIC), Mr. B. (another great leader). They always made sure that we had everything we needed to perform at our best and keep us moving forward. He was an old school "Quiet Professional." Chief Leif was stern but attentive and respectful. He genuinely cared, and that had a huge impact on me as well as the rest of the platoon, seeing that kind of leader in real life.

On our rotation from Germany to Sarajevo, we stayed in the nearby NATO headquarters with all the generals and brass in close proximity. It was boring, but the food was good. We ate in the same place all the bigwigs ate. By this time, I was already addicted to pastries, cookies, cakes—anything that was sweet, I had to have it. The problem was that we used to eat at midnight after late workouts, and the kitchen staff refused to give away any sweets that late. For midnight meals, we didn't need uniforms and were wearing civilian clothes. Per regulations, there were no pastries or sweets at midnight meals. However, one night I noticed someone with a full plate of cookies at their table in midnight rations (midrats).

I asked the kitchen personnel, "How come he gets cookies?"

"He's a general. He gets what he wants."

After a week, I got sick and tired of it, so as were checking in for another midnight meal I asked for a cake with my meal. Same excuse: no cakes for midnight meals. I looked at the kitchen staff and said: "You, go and tell your chef, that General Dzieran is here!!! I want my cakes as usual! I want my cake now, at that table!" I pointed to some random table. I was older than most of my teammates, so I figured I could get away with it—and I did.

I have never seen kitchen people moving so fast in my life. By the time I made it to the table with my meal, there was a huge platter with all assortments of cakes, cookies, and pastries. When the rest of our guys walked in, the platter full of sweets was waiting. Their eyes were huge!

"Dude, how did you pull it off?"

"I will tell you later, but for now call me General, especially when kitchen people are nearby."

From then on, we had our pastries, cakes, and cookies with every meal. I had to be careful, because every time I showed up for midnight meal, I was greeted, "Welcome, General Dzieran." I was trying to time my meals when there were no people waiting in line, so nobody would hear the "General's greetings." It worked.

While we were deployed to Europe and between our rotations to Bosnia, we also went on some training trips. One of them was training in Lorient, France.

It was a strange and disappointing trip, unfortunately. A year or two earlier, a French officer from the French Naval Commandos had joined SEAL Team Two for a brief period as part of an exchange program, and we'd done everything we could to show him a good time—we took him on the best training trips and brought him along to work out with us. We made it a point to be nice to him. He seemed to really enjoy himself, and when he returned to France, we were excited to have someone there who knew us already and would do the same with us when we visited.

That isn't what happened. When our platoon from SEAL Team Two visited the Commandos at their base, we ended up sitting at the gate waiting for over two hours. Our old acquaintance finally showed up to let us in, saying, "You SEALs have to be on your best behavior. I know you. If you destroy anything or damage our barracks in any way, you have to pay for it with your own money before we'll even let you leave the base."

We were bewildered, thinking, *What kind of welcome is that?* The exchange put us off for the whole visit, and the feeling seemed to be mutual. The French Commandos didn't want to spend time with us if they could help it.

When we did parachute jumps on the base, they decided to go up in their own plane instead of joining us in ours. On one occasion when we did go together in the same airplane, they really decided to screw us over by stalling their own jump, waiting until the last possible second to leave the plane, which meant we had to jump when we were already past the drop zone. Most of us landed in the field, outside the designated drop zone.

There's no nice way to say it: the French guys were assholes. Between ignoring us at the gate to screwing up our exercise, we were done. We went out on our own to find something more substantial to eat; the French ate like bunny rabbits compared to us, and we were starving.

A teammate who'd gone forward to do some recon came back to tell us that he'd found a place up the hill that had real stuff on the menu like meatballs and steak. We ran up there and started pigging out. The meatballs were particularly good. Then one of the other guys started reading the menu and said, "Guys, these are *goat* balls." And these weren't ground meat—we were eating actual goat testicles.

We usually ended up having to find our own ways to occupy our time while in France. These French Naval

Commandos didn't want much to do with us. One day during the trip, with nothing else better to do, we decided to go use the gym on base. When we walked in, we found the small Commando guys jumping up and down with five-pound weights, high knees, and bending round with lots of stretching. It looked like an aerobics class—they were just missing their leg warmers and leotards. This was not our type of workout. We walked straight to the weights; Chris took up a spot on a bench to lift some weights. There were maybe ten plates available in total, so he put four or five on each side. As soon as he picked it up, the bar literally bent and the plates started falling off. We started laughing as the French guys started freaking out about the damage.

As it turned out, they rarely used their heavy equipment and relied on calisthenics and more endurance-style training than lifting weights and building strength. But it meant that their gear wasn't even able to withstand a certain amount of weight, as Chris found out that day.

After that, the Commandos refused to work out at the same time as us. When we walked in, they'd stop dead in the middle of their workouts and go sit on the sidelines and just stare blankly at us for the duration of ours. It was somewhat unnerving and annoying, just a bunch of little guys sitting around staring at us while we were trying to focus on our workouts. It didn't help their nerves watching Robert doing military presses that weighed as much as the French Commandos weighed themselves.

I guess in a way it must have been a kind of culture shock to them, the ways we exercised and how we were physically strong, but it would have gone a lot better if they hadn't been assholes about it.

While stationed in Sarajevo during this second deployment, we were able to enjoy some more relaxed moments together as a team. I mean, life was pretty great, even though we were stashed away in a CONEX box behind Sarajevo's NATO HQ. We had hot food and weren't going anywhere for a minute—it was nice to stay still for a change.

Sometimes we had to join meetings with the Army officers. On one occasion, one of their officers at the briefing sized us up, and after taking a closer look at Robert, was quick to explain to Lieutenant B., our platoon OIC, that we didn't have to wear our body armor to the meetings; the building we were in was perfectly safe. Lieutenant B. turned to her and said, "They're not wearing body armor, ma'am. They're just big like that."

We were a big platoon even by SEAL standards.

☆ ☆ ☆

One of the mission highlights was when my SEAL platoon was responsible for securing the prisoner transfer of one of the war criminals to government officials who would try him at The Hague for war crimes and genocide.

We controlled the airport where this prisoner was being held. No one was getting in (or out) without our say-so. At one point, a general's car approached one of our security checkpoints and asked to enter. One of our guys had to stop him and ask for identification. The general wasn't happy about that. He was visibly bothered by having to verify who he was, especially given his rank, but he obliged. Later on, we found out that he wrote in his report on the incident that he was impressed by the SEALs' tight security and thoroughness; that we'd done a good job not letting ourselves be intimidated or letting him slide in after his little "Do you know who I am?" tirade. We had a mass murderer under our care and observation; we wouldn't have been intimidated by an admiral, nor a general.

THIRD DEPLOYMENT
BAHRAIN, 1999–2000

For my last deployment with SEAL Team Two, we deployed to the Middle East. At the beginning we stopped in Jordan and went to Petra, the ancient city carved into a mountain (and featured in the finale of *Indiana Jones and the Last Crusade*). We had Jocko Willink as our AOIC (assistant officer in charge), and Rob O'Neill, who would become one of my best friends, was in the platoon at that time.

I got to know Jocko really well. The guy is a beast. He and Chris Stroup were the strongest guys I met during my career as a Navy SEAL. Jocko, the Brazilian Jiu-Jitsu black belt, was the guy you did not want to meet in a dark alley or get on his bad side. When he showed up to our platoon, he took one look at us and said, "I'm going to choke out this entire SEAL platoon in five minutes." (It may have been ten.) We laughed it off at first, like "yeah, sure." One after another, we got onto the wrestling mat only to be choked out within seconds. This was how we all received our intro to Brazilian Jiu-Jitsu. A couple guys suddenly remembered that they had something to work on and were gone before it was their turn. Otherwise, the entire platoon, including myself, were peacefully "choked out" and had to tap out.

But then Jocko really started teaching us, and we learned from his experience.

That's one of the things that made Jocko a great officer—he taught us how to do things firsthand, never shirking the responsibility off onto someone else or doing anything less than his best. It says a lot about a leader who treats his subordinates with respect and never asks them to do anything he wouldn't do himself. I was lucky to have and know a lot of great officers and leaders like that during my time as a SEAL. Jocko didn't have to push people—he pulled people.

I became fascinated by Brazilian Jiu-Jitsu, and my long background in martial arts came in handy here. With time, I became so proficient that when we went to Kuwait later on for a break, I was choking guys out in the ring left and right. I became so strong working out with Jocko that during a sparring session with another teammate, Jocko had to step in and tell me to let him go. My teammate was tapping out.

"Drago, man, you've got to let him go!"

"Let go, man, he tapped out!"

While choking him even harder, I started arguing that he was NOT tapping out. I did not feel nor hear any tapping. They had to pry him out of my grip.

I released my sparring partner, confused. "He didn't tap out," I told them.

"Yeah, he did," Jocko said while laughing. "Did you hear that *ti, ti, ti* sound?"

I said, "Yes, what was that?"

My sparring partner eventually caught his breath. "Dude! You had me so pinned down I couldn't even move a *finger*," he said. "I was trying to say 'tap, tap, tap' but I didn't have enough air and only this *ti, ti, ti* came out before almost passing out!"

I immediately apologized. I felt awful—well, maybe a little.

But I really enjoyed Brazilian Jiu-Jitsu, which led me to want to learn even more fighting techniques from the SEALs around me, who all came from different backgrounds and disciplines. One officer, Mr. F., had been a champion high school wrestler and had kept at it all through college. He was an incredible wrestler and a great officer. I liked him a lot. One day, Jocko paired me with him to spar; I was big and strong and figured even if I didn't know the exact techniques, I'd be good at it.

Turns out I really didn't know any wrestling techniques and was not as good as I thought I was at the time. My Jiu-Jitsu adventure was just beginning. As soon as Mr. F. and I got hold of each other, I started trying to fight him. I got him in an arm lock, but then something didn't work for me the way it should. Instead of doing the arm bar, it was more like ripping his arm out of him. I pulled on his arm for a very long time, but it wasn't making him tap out. He and Jocko knew the error I was making while trying to tap him out. Jocko started laughing first, then Mr. F. started laughing too, after he realized that my arm bar was not working.

Eventually, by the sheer force (not by the technique), I made Mr. F. tap out, and as we lay on the mat, I could hear laughing off to the side.

"I thought about interrupting and giving you a pointer, but it was too much fun to watch," Jocko said.

Mr. F. went on to explain what I was doing wrong. Instead of trying to rip arms and legs off, all I had to do was bend a wrist back this way or use my center of gravity that way to take an opponent down. I was totally exhausted. Mr. F. tapped out not because of my great technique, but because I was big and heavy and was suffocating him. He could no longer breathe. To Jocko's point, Ju-Jitsu is more like a chess match, and the faster-thinking one with a better strategy will win the fight.

This deployment, coincidentally, was where I got the nickname "Drago." I got it from Chief Tony G.; the name stuck, and there are very few SEALs who even know my real name.

It was on this deployment in late 1999, that we received a briefing: we were going to be stationed in Bahrain to help enforce the oil embargo against Iraq and, if necessary, prevent illegal shipments of crude oil from that region. For years, Iraqi dictator Saddam Hussein had violated US and United Nations–imposed sanctions and was able to stockpile millions of dollars in cash to fuel his Ba'ath Party operations as a result.

Shortly after ringing in the new millennium, in early 2000, the Navy was alerted to a violation of international shipping sanctions, and our Team was called up. The target was a Russian oil tanker, the *Volgoneft-147*, which was moving through the Persian Gulf and was suspected of carrying illegal crude oil from Iraq.

Our mission was to intercept the ship before it reached another country's territorial waters. After being transferred by helicopter to a nearby destroyer, we were briefed on the situation and told to expect young Russian sailors who would be well armed and ready for a shoot-out. Rob O'Neill was a sniper on that op. He'd been part of SEAL Team Two for a while, and by that point we were very close friends. Rob was one of the reasons it was a fun deployment as well; he could play the piano, sing, dance, and kill terrorists all with the same ease. The night of the mission, around 02:00, he was the one who woke me up and said, "Drago, we got a green light, we are go." I felt much safer with him being on the mission. Rob was a great SEAL operator and a great teammate; he was someone you could really trust to watch your six. Rob later moved on to Tier One SEAL Team. He was part of the raid on Osama bin Laden, and was the one who ultimately killed that terrorist.

It was close to 03:00 or so when the selected SEALs of my platoon roped down from helicopters onto the tanker's deck. I was designated the rope master and was the last to rope. We didn't encounter much resistance, if any. We had to work quickly, though, because in three minutes the crew could reach the territorial waters of another country; if they managed to do that, the SEALs would have to jump ship in order to not cause a major international incident. So, we worked very fast—I think we had the ship under our control and moving away from international waters in about a minute or two.

After we took over the bridge, the tanker's captain began giving orders to his crew in Russian, telling them to not cooperate with us and to resist and sabotage us in any way possible. The captain was quite surprised to discover that a few of us on the Team spoke Russian: our OIC, Mr. F., Rob, and myself.

While the ship's captain was mouthing off, Mr. F. turned around to me and said, "Take care of it." I grabbed the captain by the back of the neck and marched him out onto the deck. Surrounded by SEALs, the captain tried to keep a brave face. I pointed him to a locker on the side of the stack that was barely big enough to fit a suitcase. "Keep talking and I'll stuff you into that locker for the whole trip. If you don't fit, I will make you fit!"

He stopped talking, and then spent the rest of the voyage locked in his cabin. He didn't cause any problems again.

Once it was decided that the SEALs would stay aboard for the duration of the voyage back to the port where we could safely turn the tanker over to authorities, we rotated watch on the tanker with another squad to get some rest. (We were rotating every twelve hours to keep everyone rested and alert. Just because we can stay awake for days at a time doesn't mean we have to.) When we swapped back the next afternoon, the guys on the other squad gave us hell for leaving weapons on the ship.

"What weapons?" we asked. We were totally lost. The guys from the other squad held up a huge duffel bag full of knives and other loud clinking things. We thought for a second that those weapons belonged to the Russian tanker crew and that they'd been a lot more prepared to resist capture than we'd originally thought. Until we gave the knives a closer look.

"You idiots," someone said, "those are *butter knives.*" I think there were forks in there, too.

The other guys protested, saying they could have totally been used as weapons. Jocko came over with his binoculars and said, "You guys are arguing about butter knives, but I can see safety axes still mounted above the hatches on the ship. You didn't think to grab *those?*"

When my squad returned to the tanker, we checked on the crew. They were crying and asked for their silverware back, especially their knives.

"Why do you need them?" I said. "Just eat with your hands."

"We need them because we don't have teeth!" they replied. I watched as a couple Russian men and women on board pulled their lips back and revealed toothless gums. Among the entire Russian crew, some of whom were women, there wasn't a full set of teeth between them, and the teeth they did have were in such poor condition it hurt to chew. They had no way to break their food down to swallowable pieces. So, I went to Jocko and asked him if we could call down for the silverware. The crew was so grateful when we returned the silverware to them so they could eat that they never caused any problems for us. The ship's captain, of course, remained locked up in his cabin.

The *Volgoneft-147* operation was the biggest we undertook during that deployment; other missions were much smaller and self-contained. Most of the time we were tasked with tracking smugglers, which largely consisted of us waiting around in rigid inflatable boats on the ocean at night, listening in on Filipino and Iraqi radio transmissions like they were competing oldies stations, waiting for someone to make a mistake. Most often they were just civilian fishermen passing through, and we'd sit out on the ocean all night with nothing to do but stare at the water and wait.

There was plenty of boredom in the SEALs and lots of ways to cure it. I opted to reenlist during this deployment, which gave me something to do while we bobbed up and down like apples in the Persian Gulf.

There's an old Navy SEAL/UDT custom for reenlistment of a UDT or SEAL in old traditional UDT shorts. UDT (Underwater Demolition Team) were the original SEALs, the frogmen predecessors of Navy SEALs. I was reenlisting along with one of my teammates on the same day. It was decided that we would reenlist the old way: in UDT shorts. Easier said than done. We don't use these types of shorts in SEAL Teams anymore. But, luckily, somebody on the carrier (Kennedy CV-67) had these shorts with them. We had our choice between two pairs of shorts; my teammate got to them first, and of course grabbed the bigger ones for himself. My options were to either make the squeeze or forfeit this old SEAL traditional reenlistment.

That wasn't going to happen. I squeezed into those UDT shorts and reenlisted in the old tradition, and I felt so proud of myself. If you look up pictures of me and Jocko from this period, you might find one of the photographs of me reenlisting while wearing some incredibly tight shorts on the deck of a ship. They were painful to wear and still painful to see, but what the hell. It was a once in a lifetime occasion to have the old UDT-type reenlistment. That was one of my more memorable reenlistments.

Jocko and I met up again later in 2003, when he came to Iraq as a platoon OIC. We conducted many missions together. Jocko returned again to Iraq in 2006, to Ramadi as Task Unit Commander for SEAL Team Three. Under Jocko's leadership, Task Unit Bruiser became the most highly decorated US special operations unit of the Iraq war.

Bahrain was a great place to celebrate the new millennium. We had a great time hanging out on the base and walking around the city, going to bars, and meeting all kinds of people. I didn't have a lot of money and neither did many of the other guys. As SEALs, we got paid regular Navy pay, plus specialty pay for qualifications like demolition, dive, jump, and language proficiency (I got bonus pay, since I spoke Polish and Russian), and it all added up, but we weren't swimming in cash.

So, we had to get creative during our downtime.

At one bar we liked to hang out at, there was a glass partition between the bar and what looked like a ballroom. One night, on the other side of the partition, two women were slamming back cocktail after cocktail. I was impressed and thirsty—I didn't drink a lot of neat liquor or beer at that time but preferred what are considered more "girly" drinks. I was out of money and drooling over those amazing-looking cocktails, so I went and collected a bunch of straws. While my teammates drank, I discovered a crack in the partition and started pushing the straws together from end to end to build a single Super Straw. I pushed that through the partition crack and got it into the closest cocktail glass and started drinking. The women didn't notice at first, so I had a couple of drinks on them. But then some of my fellow SEALs spotted my shenanigans and joined in on it. What a money saver! Unfortunately, on my side of the partition there were now a bunch of SEALs trying for a free drink on those women's tab. It was not too difficult to notice that something weird was going on, and we got caught! We got kicked out of that bar for that, but it was worth it for good drinks and a great story.

At the end of my third deployment, we were taken to Spain to await transport back to the United States. This was a great change of pace. Instead of having to stay aboard a carrier or on a base, we got put up in a hotel in Rota, near Cádiz. It was absolutely beautiful—I could take one step out of my room and be on the beach.

All in all, it was an awesome deployment.

Upon our return, many of us were assigned to SEAL Team Four. The move was not a big deal—all we needed to do was grab our gear from the lockers at SEAL Team Two, and march to another building where SEAL Team Four was located. Fifteen minutes later, we were at SEAL Team Four.

FOURTH DEPLOYMENT – TERRORIST TERRORIZER CENTRAL AND SOUTH AMERICA, 2003, AND IRAQ, 2003–2004

What was waiting for me back home, though, wasn't great. My marriage had fallen apart while I was overseas. It's no secret that life as a Navy SEAL puts a serious strain on your personal life, family, and marriage. My life was no different than many of my SEAL teammates. Most of our time is divided with six months or more for platoon workup, then six months deployment overseas. There never really is any time at home. Once the divorce was final, I lost my home along with my family. I was financially broken, too. Without the structure and distraction of being deployed, I was getting myself into a lot of trouble back in Virginia Beach.

Eventually I ended up in a new platoon doing another pre-deployment work-up. Our deployment was scheduled to Puerto Rico. That was our launchpad. I returned to the only place where I knew I could trust the people I was with—my fellow SEALs, who were like family to me and whom I knew better than my real brother.

I was still struggling with some behavioral issues while stationed in South America. I think I am still the only guy to get written up for being "mean" to my new platoon to the point that—per my chief—some of the guys didn't want to ride in the same vehicle with me (mostly new guys). I tried to play nicer, and I devoted myself to doing my job well and accomplishing all my tasks.

Three months into my South American deployment, my chief, Nicky B., called me into his office. At first, I was expecting another reprimand, but instead he told me that because I spoke Polish, I was being ordered to Baghdad to help with the integration of Polish Special Forces (GROM), which were operating with the SEAL Teams from the West Coast. I was assigned as a liaison officer, tasked with helping the GROM coordinate and work with the SEALs on combat missions in Iraq.

Chief Nicky B. was one the chiefs who played a key role in me getting my career back on track and helping me while I was going through the turbulent part of life after the divorce. I will always remember Chief Nicky (today Warrant Officer (ret.)) as the chief to whom I owe so much. Chief

Nicky's legacy is also known to my children. When the guys were complaining about me being "mean," Chief had me write an essay on what it means to be a SEAL and a team player. I have effectively applied this technique for teaching my children how to reflect on better ways to complete tasks that they may have had issues with. My older boys wrote many essays. The same son who wrote multiple safety essays on the proper handling of fires and fire control is the one who joined the US Marines and worked as fire support where his main job was to set fires and blow things up.

I was very happy with this assignment. When I told my teammates that I was going to war, they were pissed and a bit jealous. SEALs are an aggressive bunch, so they were rightfully upset that I was going to go get experience in Iraq while they had to stay behind waiting for their turn. I knew I was lucky. I remember feeling similarly when I was a Fucking New Guy watching the veteran SEALs with envy as they drank and told stories and trained for their next mission. But I wasn't mad at them for getting to go to war; I was envious of their experiences and wanted the same for myself.

The way it was explained to me was that I would still be operating on a six-month deployment schedule, so I would be going to Iraq for three months. After that, I would return to SEAL Team Four at Little Creek, join a new platoon, and continue with work-up for the next deployment. I was excited, and off I went. It was a strange feeling as I had to fly a civilian aircraft to Bahrain first, with all my gear and all my guns. I had to check them in on the flight like any other passenger. My military deployment was starting from a civilian airport, in my civilian clothes.

The first thought I had when I landed in Baghdad was: *It's so goddamned hot.* I had just been spending all my time in humid Puerto Rico and South America, and even before that I had never encountered that kind of extreme dry heat. When I walked off the plane, I thought I'd stepped into a jet blast, the pressure and heat was so intense. I was stepping side to side to try and get away from it, only to realize that it was actually the wind.

From there, I was taken to the SEAL compound, Camp Pozzi, where I quickly acclimated and got to work. For those first three months in Iraq, I didn't hear from my commanders in Little Creek once. I figured they were busy, so I chose not to bother them. It reached the point that when I was notified by an officer in Iraq that my platoon was leaving South America back to the United States, I decided to just stay in Iraq since no one had reached out to me about coming back and because I loved what I was doing. I didn't want to go back. I felt really at home doing what I had been training for years to do.

My job was to help coordinate missions and facilitate communication between the SEAL Teams and Polish Special Forces, using my Polish and English language skills to do so. My commanders were wary about sending me on Direct Action missions incorporated in the GROM assault element structure. They were worried about my safety. I refused to stay back and asked to be allowed to join GROM's assault element during Direct Action missions.

GROM operators are Tier One operators and some of the best in the world. They are often deployed in a variety of special operations and unconventional warfare roles. I deeply enjoyed my time with GROM, and, of course, I welcomed a chance to fight side by side with Polish commandos.

The roots of GROM can be traced to the Second World War and a small group of specially selected soldiers who volunteered to serve beyond the front lines in German-occupied and then Soviet-occupied Europe. After training in Great Britain, these commandos parachuted into occupied Poland to lead the largest underground army in occupied Europe, the Polish Home Army (Armia Krajowa—AK). Today, the GROM unit is proudly named after these commandos—the Cichociemni.

The concept of Polish Special Forces (GROM) was created in the early 1990s by Polish General Petelicki, who is the founder and creator of this highly trained commando unit. The US cooperation and help in creating this premiere unit started after Poles carried out Operation Simoom (in Polish: Samum) where Polish intelligence agents rescued six CIA and DIA officers from Iraq in a top-secret operation in 1990. France and Great Britain refused to help with such a dangerous operation—only Poland agreed. The operation was very risky because if the cover were to be blown, all operatives were likely to be killed. This daring exploit was masterminded by Gen. Gromosław Czempiński, a man who for twenty years had battled the CIA as a Warsaw Pact spy. This was one of three covert Polish operations during the Gulf War that aided the Allied war efforts. Polish agents carried to freedom fifteen more foreign personnel (mostly British). At the same time, Polish intelligence provided the United States with detailed maps of Baghdad and intel about military installation throughout Iraq.

Poles had been trained by the Americans and the British for years. They were familiar with our operating procedures, used similar tactics, and were equipped with modern (Western) equipment. The GROM easily integrated with our SEAL platoons while operating in Iraq, because from the very inception they were created to model the elite US Special Forces and perform to American standards. This unit never had the baggage of Communist military structures nor the Communist approach to combat. They are highly skilled and experienced warriors.

Many of our missions involved eliminating al-Qaeda insurgents and other suspected terrorists in cities and rural areas across Iraq. Since I was also a Naval Special Warfare Lead Breacher, I was most often first in line as the lead breacher during these operations. I was responsible for gaining access to the structures, creating entry points through doors, walls, or other obstacles using explosives or sometimes manual tools, which allowed us to get inside quickly. It was very dangerous work, but a lot of fun.

This is where I met Tej for the first time. He was attached to SEAL Team Five and had already been in Iraq for some time. We immediately became good friends, and we are still today.

We were big and heavy, and because of our size, we were often designated as prisoner handlers to haul terrorists from the targets. This is where I devised a kind of crash course in English for terrorists, otherwise known as "Drago's Accelerated English Course for Terrorists." Working together, Tej and I applied this technique very effectively. My motto was, "Give me ten minutes with a terrorist who doesn't speak English and by the end he'll come out speaking better English than I do." It always worked.

Our English classes worked so well that during one of the Direct Action (DA) missions, we were talking to an Agency officer while the target was already secured. The officer was pleasantly surprised with how quickly Tej and

I were able to make the terrorist speak English. She was trying to get information out of a prisoner who kept saying he didn't speak English, stalling for time. We asked her to leave us for ten minutes so we could "speak to him and provide him with 'Drago's Accelerated English Course for Terrorists,' and 'teach him more English.'" She came back ten minutes later and explained how easy it had been to talk with him. (After only one class with Tej and me, the terrorist's English was almost perfect).

The officer kept writing, writing, and writing; Tej and I mused that this guy definitely started speaking good English—with an even better accent than mine. It almost made me jealous. At one point, she had to stop his rambling and run to get another legal pad so she could keep writing. That officer told us afterward that she'd been in the country for three months trying to gather intel, and she got more in those ten minutes than she had in all that time. Tej and I loved our jobs.

In my opinion, the best way to win the war on terror is to terrorize the terrorists. When I went to Iraq, I did not go there to win hearts and minds. I went there to kill and terrorize the terrorists. My only regret from war is that we did not kill more of them.

☆ ☆ ☆

What makes urban warfare so complicated and dangerous is that it's three-dimensional warfare, which means attacks can come from above, below, or directly next to you. Enemies can be lurking anywhere and behind almost anything. We never knew what we were going to find—or who we were going to encounter—during Direct Action missions. The presence of civilians and the complexity of urban terrain only complicated things, and we often encountered booby traps, snipers, and belowground infrastructures that were extremely difficult and treacherous to navigate.

There were plenty of places for terrorists to hide, and it was our mission to find them and take them into custody or kill them if necessary. At times, I felt like government customer service, except my customers were always wrong and I got to kill them.

I learned firsthand—and very quickly—just how evil this enemy was. Al-Qaeda liked to keep women and children in the front rooms of their buildings as a buffer between them and any explosions, and they often used them as human shields during our assaults. This is how inhumane and ruthless the terrorists we hunted were. Not only that, but it was cowardly, being willing to sacrifice their own women and children to keep themselves safe.

Although our missions were very dangerous, a couple of them turned out to be rather humorous and memorable.

During one nighttime assault, our intelligence indicated that there were two large dogs in the backyard of one of the targets we were supposed to assault. Two of my team members were responsible for quietly neutralizing the dogs so their barking wouldn't warn the terrorists of our presence. When one of the GROM guys climbed a ladder to the top of the ten-foot-high concrete wall surrounding the house, I heard him say in Polish, "I can see the two dogs. Damn, these things are fucking huge!"

I immediately thought to myself, *Damn, that's not good.* It was eerily quiet, no barking, so the entire assault element decided to climb over the wall. As I straddled the top of the wall, I looked through my night vision goggles at the ground to try and spot these giant dogs. Turns out, the dogs hadn't been barking because we were so quiet—the "dogs" were actually skinny cows! We reached the ground, blew the front door off the building, and captured the terrorists without firing a shot that night.

During the post-mission briefing, I noticed the GROM commando who had made the call about the two dogs sitting at a table, his head bowed a little. His commanders were showing him flash cards with crudely drawn pictures of animals on them.

"What's this?" they asked him.

"A dog," he said, obviously embarrassed.

"What's this?" they asked, pulling out another card.

"A chicken," he replied.

"And this?"

"A cow."

I backed out of the room quietly, smothering my laughter behind a fist. The GROM are perfectionists, and they were serious about making sure that that kind of mistake never happened again. I'm sure that guy never again mistook a cow for a dog.

During another mission, this one to capture an Iraqi Air Force general with proven involvement in various terrorist attacks, our intelligence indicated that he was hiding in a building with solid doors that would be very difficult to breach. A standard compound, a standard mission.

As we approached the house in the dark, I noticed the doors were strong, but not quite as thick as anticipated. I had initially calibrated charges for a stronger door. I knew if I breached the door per the original intel, the explosives would do more damage than expected and potentially kill anyone inside. Familiar with the uncertainty of urban warfare, I was prepared for the situation and immediately replaced the original breaching charge with a smaller one that would get the job done. I was unaware that while I was breaching the door, the target was standing on the other side of the door with his hand on the doorknob and his ear against the door, trying to listen to what was happening outside. He obviously couldn't hear me, because after I detonated the smaller charge, we found the general standing in the doorway, holding only the doorknob. He didn't look severely injured at first, but he was obviously dazed and confused by the blast. I got him on the ground and cuffed him with zip-ties, but as I cinched the plastic around his wrists, I had a hard time understanding why the general had three hands. On closer inspection, I realized that the hand that had been holding on to the doorknob had been split clean up the middle. In the dark, it had the effect of making it feel like the guy had fifteen fingers and three hands. Luckily, the zip ties worked well as a tourniquet.

Before leaving the area, the Iraqi general asked the GROM soldiers a question in clear, perfect Polish. He asked if they were from Poland, to which the GROM guys replied yes.

The general's eyes lit up. Even as I held him by the wrists, he shouted to them, "Hey, get me out of here! The Americans are after me. Get me out of here! I have money. I have whatever you want."

The GROM commander with us asked him to confirm his name.

"Yeah, that's me," the general replied.

The Polish commander looked at me and said, "Drago, get on the radio and let your SEAL commander know that we have the son of a bitch."

The Iraqi general started crying and screaming in perfect Polish, "You fucking bastards! How can you do this to me?"

The Iraqi general spoke fluent Polish because Polish Armed Forces had trained the Iraqi Air Force to fly jets during the 1970s and '80s, back when there was a lot of crossover between the USSR and Western Asia (in particular during the Soviet-Afghan war).

On most of our Direct Action missions we encountered civilians including women and children on target, most often sleeping in the rooms adjacent to the doors being breached. It was imperative not to blow the doors off the hinges; instead, we needed to blast them open while only stunning the people inside. Doors blown off the hinges could create another problem for the assault element by blocking or obstructing access to the target or injuring innocent children who were often present. We were successful.

During this time in Iraq (circa 2003), I devised a new breaching charge that allowed us to explosively breach obstacles with minimal fragmentation. This prevented injuries to non-combatants, innocent civilians who often found themselves in the crossfire. The charge was safer to use for us as well, as it allowed a smaller standoff from the explosion and less fragmentation. This charge was based on a principle that was different than the standard breaching charge principles we learned in breaching school. This newly devised breaching charge became widely used by SEAL Teams in breaching operations throughout Iraq. I also started using different tactics from those taught in the breaching school. I was one of the proponents of those tactics modifications that were eventually accepted into the breaching curriculum.

Additionally, I created a database containing all the pertinent information for each breach operation. I consider these safer breaching charges and tactics my biggest contribution to the SEAL Teams.

After I returned from this deployment, I was ordered to meet with Tier One SEAL Team Breachers and brief them on all this new information. I dressed up in my best cammies and drove to their secure compound where I was ushered inside. I shared my breaching techniques and the new breaching charges information and showed images of the target before the breach and after each breach. I also provided them with my compilation of all the breaching data for Iraq. It was a great honor.

It was while working in Iraq as an NSW Lead Breacher that I began to really notice the impact of close proximity explosions from the breaching charges. I started to notice some memory issues, problems with my vision, and balance issues. This didn't scare me as much as it made me very aware of what I was doing. I made it a point to be extremely focused during missions so I wouldn't forget or mistake anything after.

Soon, my three-month stay in Iraq became four. Then five. By the time I'd reached nearly nine months in-country, I began to wonder if SEAL Team Four had forgotten I ever existed. My girlfriend, who I'd met shortly after my divorce, sent me an email right before Christmas. I had recently told her I would be back in three months, and she'd written to tell me that this SEAL life—my life—wasn't for her. She said that she "could have handled three months. But six was pushing it, and nine was too much." All of my clothes and belongings would be packed in my Jeep and parked in front of her apartment for me to pick up when I got back. She finished by saying she was going to a Christmas party with someone she'd met while I was away.

I agreed. We were done.

The West Coast platoon I'd been with in Iraq while working with GROM had since rotated out and others had come in. Still, no one said anything about my extended stay.

I didn't plan on flagging the issue; however, one day when I broke my night vision goggles, I had no choice but to call back to command for a new set of NVGs. I had been borrowing the equipment from the West Coast platoons that had been rotating in and out the past nine months; each platoon only had so many resources and supplies, and if I broke something of theirs, that was a bigger issue for them than it was for me. So, they finally had to cut me off.

There was nothing for me to do but call my command, SEAL Team Four, who hadn't heard from me since leaving for Iraq. I managed to get in touch with an FNG at the armory and told him I needed a set of NVGs sent to me in Baghdad.

"Who is this?"

"It's Drago."

"Okay, Drago, one set of NVGs. Do you want a suicidal bomb vest to go with that?"

I was stunned. "What are you talking about?"

"You can barely speak English, dude! Are you an Iraqi trying to get yourself some cool gear on the SEALs' tab?"

Turns out, the new guy thought I was an Iraqi terrorist. An Iraqi terrorist who somehow managed to get a direct line to SEAL Team Four's armory in Little Creek, Virginia. I had to threaten to kill the dumb kid for him to put me through to the master chief, who was thrilled to hear from me.

"Drago! How are you? How is everything?"

"Awesome, Master Chief, I'm still in Iraq..."

It was crickets on the other line. Finally, I heard the master chief clear his throat.

"*How long* have you been there?"

"Going on nine months now."

Master Chief spat out a hearty "Oh, shit!" and told me to hold on while he got the executive officer on the other line. After a few moments, the XO's voice came through.

"We need you to come back. SEAL Team ▉ is about to deploy, and we're next up, so you need to come and meet your new platoon and get ready to deploy on schedule with your Team."

By that time, Camp Pozzi had become my home. I was so immersed in the combat operations there that it had become my reality, my home, where I felt good. This was a home where I fit well and belonged. I remember sometimes daydreaming about the life in America, but it had become more like a surreal fairy tale that I could reach only with my memories. It felt more like how other people think about stories they read in books. The life in America seemed so distant and almost unreal. The "real" was here, in Baghdad, in combat. And I loved it.

☆ ☆ ☆

After almost a year-long deployment, I came home from Iraq.

It was still wintertime, and cold, cloudy days in Virginia Beach were common. When I landed in Norfolk, Virginia, two other military personnel and I walked through the door, but I was the only one with a stack of cruise boxes and bags full of SEAL gear. It was early afternoon, and after the customs check, I carried my belongings to the curb. It was Saturday and quiet at the military side of the airport. I felt relieved, and it dawned on me that I was safe now. I felt like a balloon where all the air escaped. I realized how tired I was. The two other personnel were picked up by their families and left. The airport was closed; it was the weekend and they didn't expect any other traffic. The guard asked me if I needed any help. I said, "No, thank you, I have a truck with my people coming to pick me up." I sat on my cruise boxes, wrapped myself in the poncho, and expecting the truck to show up any time now, relaxed. I fell asleep.

I woke up violently shivering. Above me was this huge fluorescent light that buzzed constantly. It was getting dark and I was still sitting on the pile of my gear and cruise boxes. Nobody showed up. My cell phone was dead, and the airport was closed. Not much longer and I would be hypothermic—I needed to do something. Knocking on the airport doors did nothing. It seemed like nobody was there. I had to get to the phone. I saw a garbage can in the concrete encasing and determined that I would throw it through the window to get to the phones. As I heaved it up and was about to throw it, a person showed up on the other side of the doors. I pointed out to the stack of my gear at the curb and asked for the phone. He let me in.

Wow! The place felt so warm—what an awesome feeling! There wasn't anybody at the SEAL Team Four building, so I called NSW Group Two quarterdeck and asked them for a ride back to the Teams.

You can imagine my surprise when they responded with confusion.

"What do you mean no one came to pick you up? Who are you?"

"I'm Drago, I just came back from Iraq and I need a ride," I replied.

"Dude, we don't have anybody in Iraq. What accent is that anyway? Stop calling or we will call the police." *Click.*

I called again and asked to speak to the OOD (officer of the deck). After a while he came on the line, and he vaguely remembered seeing something about my arrival in documents. I could hear him shuffling papers. It got quiet, and with apologies, he informed me that it was overlooked—he would send a truck immediately.

A support tech from SEAL Team Four came within the hour and helped me load up my gear into the back of his truck. Finally, I was back in the SEAL Team Four compound, checking in my guns and the rest of my gear. What a relief. When walking by the now empty quarterdeck, I helped myself to keys for one of the trucks, just in case. As we walked out of the Team area, the tech who brought me in shut the door, jumped in his truck, and started to leave. My plan was to spend the night in the SEAL Team Four compound and come up with a plan in the morning on what to do next. I asked for the code to get inside. He replied: "I can't—you SEALs aren't allowed to sleep at the team compound after hours anymore."

He took off, leaving me in the front of the compound. My cell phone was dead, deactivated, and I had no means to get inside. I found the truck matching the key that I took from the empty quarterdeck.

I drove to the ATM on base. My ex-wife had previously emptied my bank accounts and the divorce was still being paid for, so I had a little over $25 in the bank and pulled out $20. I was hungry too, so having only $20 didn't give me much of a choice. I drove myself to the local IHOP. Besides, I loved (still do) IHOP's cheese blintz. It reminds me of the pancakes my mom used to make in Poland. To IHOP I went.

My first night back in America after months spent away on my first deployment to Iraq, and I spent the night at an IHOP in Virginia Beach, Virginia. (About as American as it gets, my wife tells me.) Looking back on it now, it actually seems fitting. I remember the smell of fresh coffee and food being cooked. I felt awesome again. I asked for coffee and my cheese blintz. I ate all of it and drank my coffee dry. Suddenly I felt tired and safe. That was a strange feeling, the realization that there I was in the safest place in the world, my home, back in America. I slowly faded away, and fell asleep. I was woken up shortly by the security officer, who asked me if everything was okay. I said yes, thank you. I asked if I could hang out there for a while.

He looked at me carefully, then asked, "Did the bitch kick you out?"

I got confused for a second—what is he asking me about? But then quickly replied: "Yes, the bitch kicked me out."

He said, "You can hang out here, just don't cause any problems." I thanked him.

I was back home, in America.

FIFTH DEPLOYMENT
IRAQ, 2004

In the morning, I drove back to Little Creek. As I pulled into SEAL Team Four, I could already see some SEALs going in and out of the building. One of the guys saw me and called, "Hey Drago! Good to see you, come on in! We've heard stories about you."

I told the guys the story of what had happened the night before. At the end of it, we all laughed, and they told me I should have just pounded on the back door of the main building. "We're all sleeping in there. We know we're not supposed to, but fuck that, we need to stay somewhere. We're staying here."

I couldn't find myself in Virginia Beach; I didn't have family there anymore. When the opportunity came about to go back to Iraq, I was excited and jumped on the opportunity.

I was missing Iraq, I was missing combat, and I missed the work I had been doing there. I was told that I could join them for a couple of weeks and once again act as liaison with GROM. I'd be helping them out since the new team hadn't had any previous experience working with Polish Special Forces.

Two weeks went by, and I was expecting the call from command to return to Virginia. It never came. Two weeks became four weeks, and then four weeks became four months. After my first extra-long stint in Iraq, the saying went, "No news from Drago is good news."

It was interesting to see how the methods and tactics used in Iraq were evolving over time. Soon after arriving, the SEAL Team I was deployed with was tasked with providing security for the new Iraqi government officials; they left, and I stayed behind with GROM and kept conducting Direct Action raids. Eventually, I even ended up coordinating between GROM and US Marines who'd recently arrived in Iraq. (My GROM friends had initially protested, saying they only wanted to work with SEALs, but I told them, "The Marines are as good as we are. These guys are awesome, and you will love working with them." And they did!) It was great to work with these Marines and observe their dedication and their precise execution of the missions.

After four months with no word from my original command, I finally got a call. They ordered me to come back and reintegrate with my SEAL Team Four platoon, because *we* would be deploying to Iraq in a short time as we were next in line, after the SEAL Team currently there. I didn't have much say in the matter at that point, so I got on a cargo plane and flew back to Virginia, where I immediately dove into training with my platoon, getting to know them and learning how to work together. A few months later, I was back in Iraq, doing the same missions but in a different region.

Between my first deployment to Iraq in 2003 and my latest in 2005, I had spent the better part of two years in-country.

SIXTH DEPLOYMENT
BAGHDAD, IRAQ, 2005

By my last deployment in 2005, things had changed considerably since I'd first come to Iraq in 2003. In the wake of 9/11, the bureaucracy had intensified, and the war was now being fought largely by the Army and Marines. Even our pre-raid briefs—when we received last-minute intel and reviewed dossiers, maps, and recon photos—had become longer and longer. This wasn't the old days of maps on walls and physical files either; everything was digital now. We called it Death by PowerPoint. It seemed like we were briefing for the sake of the brief in order to brief *more*. If that sounds confusing, trust me, it was. I still believe to this day that it was an Army requirement that we were being forced to adopt. Then the missions became scarcer, and we were no longer assaulting targets every night.

The intel was also coming in less frequently and less accurately. On the increasingly rare occasions we hit a hideout, it had often already been abandoned by the time we arrived. The enemy also learned, and we often found the house set up with propane tanks by the possible entry points. The new breaching charges were handy, and due to their design, they tended to not affect the propane tanks set up by the door. I am aware of an occasional breaching charge that set off such propane tanks, but the tanks didn't explode and produced only a funnel of fire that was quickly extinguished. The new charges worked well for us.

The primary mission of my last deployment was to act as security for Iraqi officials. I was on the bodyguard detail for one of the top Iraqi government officials who had been instated following the fall of Saddam Hussein in April 2003. Wherever he went, we went. We'd clear houses, office buildings, even bathrooms before he walked into them. And it was still so goddamned hot and boring. Those missions were called "no fail missions."

The heat would have been tolerable if the work hadn't been so boring. I would try to bow out of it and go on Direct

Action (DA) missions instead. DA missions meant getting to do the stuff you were trained to do instead of babysitting a grown man all day long. I was accused of breaking off and going on my own private missions, which was only kind of true—I wasn't just walking off into the desert on my own. The DA missions were conducted from an entirely different base, so I would seize every opportunity to visit that base and hide out there until I was sent out on a DA mission.

But soon even those lost their appeal. The bureaucratic chain of command began requiring extensive after-action reports about SEAL missions. Paperwork is awful no matter where you do it. Not only that, but doing what they asked—writing down every detail of my missions as a SEAL—would have been a sure way to ruin my own career. Because of reports of prisoners being tortured at Abu Ghraib prison, the military was really cracking down on everyone to make sure everything was legal and followed protocol. In the SEAL Teams, of course we have to ensure we follow protocol and stay within the law, but sometimes we do push the envelope to get the job done. Some senior leaders and politicians do not like that, and over time, military leaders create and enforce regulations that are stricter than the law and more rigid than the legal rules of engagement. Eventually, the warfighters are barely able to operate effectively. Sometimes it seemed as if the American government would rather protect terrorists than protect our brave American servicemen and women.

But, I am a SEAL, a military man, and an American, so I did my job to the best of my ability while following the restrictions placed upon us. That is our duty.

★ CHAPTER SEVENTEEN ★

HOMECOMING

COMING BACK FROM MY LAST deployment, I got my orders to breaching school in Virginia. Initially I was excited about it, but as my health issues started surfacing, I wanted to stay away from explosions of any kind. Any kind of loud noise caused me a terrible headache, I was getting nose-bleeds for no reason, and I was unable to read. I could read a paragraph and not remember what I read at the beginning of the same paragraph. Reading itself became a chore, as the lines and letters were jumping and mixing together. I knew that something was wrong with me. I asked for a change to my orders.

It was not easy, especially considering that the common presumption was that I belonged in the breaching school. After many shenanigans and after calling a friend of mine, Chief B., with whom I was conducting many DA raids in Iraq, and who was at that time a SEAL detailer in Millington, Tennessee, I was able to change my orders, and I was assigned to the Naval Special Warfare Center as a SEAL instructor. I moved to Coronado, California. I was forced to cobble together a living situation as soon as I got there. I found a small apartment not too far from base that worked pretty well.

However, it seemed this great fit might have a ghost problem I wasn't expecting. It became a regular occurrence that at exactly 2:05 a.m., I would go from sound asleep to suddenly wide awake and alert. When I asked my teammates what they thought was the problem, the consensus was the apartment must be haunted by a ghost. We could not see any other explanation. It surely was not me. I found out that I am scared of ghosts! I thought about moving out and finding a different apartment, but it was impossible to find anything reasonably priced in Coronado, so I was out of luck and stuck with my ghost.

At that time, I did not understand or appreciate the impact of combat and how close proximity exposure to blasts from my breaching work could affect my body. It was not until I was out of the Teams and retired that I could reflect more on that situation—and many others—to appreciate how insidious war can be for a person's health and well-being. Also, with time, more information became available about traumatic brain injury (TBI).

After many years as a Navy SEAL, always on the move and never setting down roots in any one place, I realized that I was finally at a point in my life where I could begin thinking about meeting someone, getting married, and raising a family. I wanted to live out my American dream in America.

During years of deployments, side missions, rest periods, and general travel and adventure, a lot of things tend to fall to the wayside. For some guys it could be their family or friends; other guys cut out things from their diet or lifestyle. We all had our ways of dealing with SEAL life. Some of the sacrifices we make are big, and some are very small and unremarkable.

In my case, I somewhat lost my fashion sense. I had no need of it when I lived in my gear for months at a time and I had perfectly good basic civvies back home: mostly jeans and black T-shirts and one decent suit. A lot of what I owned dated back to the '70s. (Clothes used to be made to last.) I was told by some of my teammates that I needed new clothes if I wanted to have a social life outside the Teams in Coronado. In those days, if you showed up to a formal event in jeans and a T-shirt, you were considered underdressed.

So my friends took me shopping. They gave me a little California makeover of sorts. My heavily used and threadbare stuff went in the garbage. They knew I wanted to meet a girl who I could date. They had also seen my dressing habits: blue jeans and a black T-shirt for everyday wear. When I wanted to look fancy, I wore a blue T-shirt and black jeans. White socks and tennis shoes completed my wardrobe.

Fellow SEALs saw my struggle. At one time or another, some of them were invited to some nice parties, even with Hollywood personalities. I was invited sometimes too, but one particular time, when we rang the bell, some prune-looking old lady opened the door with a big smile. The other Team guys proceeded to enter the door, until the old lady laid her eyes on me. The smile disappeared; her face wrinkled up even more when she pointed a finger at me and asked incredulously, "Who is that?"

She was told that I was with them. Before she kicked us all out and shut the door, I could hear her screeching that it was not a drug party or bum party. We were left in front of the shut door. So much for our mingling with elites. I felt very sorry for my friends—I didn't mean to get them into hot water. I offered to leave my friends at the door to try and get into the party, and I would go to a bar in San Diego. But the sound answer was *Fuck the ole lady, we will all go to the bar and party together.*

The consensus was that I definitely needed some decent clothes, and we'd mount an expedition to a mall, where they would pick the clothes for me. Of course, I was paying. I was very grateful to them. The next weekend we made the trip to shoe and clothing stores and I was finally dressed up in decent clothes. I will be forever grateful to my teammates for this. Now I felt like there was not a single girl who could resist my charm (and my new clothes).

By 2007, I was approaching retirement from the Teams. I didn't have a home or family other than my SEAL brothers. I dated during that time, meeting lots of women who I liked but couldn't see myself building a life with. I knew I wanted someone who was beautiful, funny, and passionate about things, someone who really wanted a partnership like I did. There were always plenty of "frog hogs" around (a very unflattering name for the women who like to hang around bars near naval bases hoping to catch a Navy SEAL). But I'd been down that road before, and I knew it wouldn't lead me to the future I wanted for myself.

With the help of my SEAL brothers, I turned to online dating services to try and find the woman of my dreams. Trying to flirt online was strange, but not everyone else seemed to find it as awkward as I did. Conversations usually started with a "wink" or "poke" on a dating website. After some small talk back and forth, if the interest was mutual, I might have shared emails or a phone call with the woman on the other end of the line.

One woman I met seemed like a great catch. She had posted beautiful photographs on her profile and shared a lot of interesting stories with me over email. We eventually agreed to talk on the phone. The moment she heard my thick accent for the first time, she told me that she was going to hang up and call the FBI. She completely blew up at me and demanded to know how I ended up on a dating website called "American Singles" when I obviously wasn't one. I hung up on her instead.

I was undeterred. Despite a few more setbacks, I took one more chance at finding love online. A woman I'd seen on a site had caught my eye—she had dark hair, a big smile, and seemed interesting—so I sent her a wink. I checked the next morning and saw that I hadn't received an answer. So, I sent another wink. No answer again. A third wink and a few days later, I finally received a message from her.

We emailed back and forth for a couple of days, and I was totally charmed. Her name was Rachel. She was everything I was looking for in a woman and a partner: beautiful, witty, smart, and successful in her own right. She was much younger than me, which made me a little nervous. What if she thought I was too old for her? On the advice of my teammates, I had taken a few years off my real age for the dating site. Even then I still barely fit her preferred age range (I found this out later).

I didn't want to risk losing her, so I asked some of my SEAL teammates to help me write love letters to her. Lucky for me, Rachel found the first letter acceptable enough to respond. She wrote back, and we proceeded to mail each other letters. Mine were written by my fellow SEAL brothers—whoever I could grab and drag to the computer was my scribe.

After a few weeks, my SEAL buddies were somewhat tired of writing my love letters and encouraged me to write my own. They said I could easily borrow from previous letters, copy and paste, no problem. Even as they pushed me into the deep end, they assured me I would be okay and that they were standing by to help if needed. I was terrified—my English was still pretty rough and not what fit a subtle and gentle conversation about feelings. What if she stopped responding because of the change?

Later, Rachel would go on to tell me that when she read my first unassisted letter, she was convinced I had been high on drugs or blackout drunk when I wrote it because it was so messy and unintelligible. Because of that, she immediately stopped communicating with me and closed her account on American Singles. The only reason she reopened it—the only reason we're together now—was because the American Singles site was so sorry for the poor experience, they offered her another thirty-day subscription free of charge. I remember sitting alone in my apartment feeling very gloomy when Rachel reappeared on the site. I was so excited to see her again!

After some desperate pleading over online messaging, she reluctantly agreed to talk to me on the phone. When Rachel heard my thick accent, she laughed.

"Now it makes sense!"

"What makes sense?" I asked.

She told me how she'd thought I was out of my mind drunk when I wrote that letter. "I thought you were only writing me when you were drunk and I tried to cancel my profile. I am so glad to hear your accent and that you're not drunk!"

I met Rachel in person about two months later. It felt like an eternity. She came to visit me in San Diego. Being mindful of my previous "dating" experiences, I asked a fellow SEAL to come with me and assist in bailing me out if Rachel turned out to be a catfish or had otherwise lied about herself online. I had her picture and a flower. The flower I kept hidden in my Jeep, just in case I had to make a last-minute escape.

I had no reason to worry, though. My teammate and I both recognized her as she came down on an escalator at the San Diego airport.

"Holy shit, Drago!" my buddy exclaimed. "She is too young! Did you rob the cradle or something? How did you pull that off?"

I laughed and replied, "You guys wrote the love letters, I lied about my age. It worked."

My buddy threw up his hands and, laughing, turned around to leave. "Whatever, dude. She's hot, I'm out."

Now really nervous, I approached the escalator to wait for her near the bottom. When she walked up to me, I was scared out of my wits. I extended my hand to her, stiff as a board from head to toe, and muttered, "Hi. I'm Thomas."

Rachel looked at me with a twinkle in her eye, and she replied breezily, "Thomas, it is nice to meet you. But I didn't fly all the way across the United States to shake your hand. Give me a hug!"

Holy shit! I melted and leaned in to give her a real Drago hug.

I was in heaven, until she pulled back to get a better look at me. She paused for a second. "I know you!" she said.

I had been in dozens if not hundreds of combat situations by that point. I was a veteran Navy SEAL! But if I'm being honest, in that moment, I was instantly gripped by pure fear. For some SEALs, having a girl you don't know or remember come up and say that she remembers you could be a very scary experience. All I could think about was whether I had met her before and, if so, if I had been mean to her. Or maybe she'd heard about me from somewhere and decided she disliked me already! First impressions are very important, and that was a terrifying moment.

Rachel went on to explain that we had crossed paths years prior, back in 1997 when I visited Langley Air Force Base with my SEAL platoon for HAPS training (High Altitude Parachute Simulation). She was an Air Force Academy graduate, stationed there as an Aerospace Physiologist, training aircrew members on high altitude threats. What a relief! Turns out she was the lead instructor who provided the academics for our HAPS training at the physiology unit. She also was one of the inside observers who participated in the "chamber flight" for our certification. They stick air crew members, or in our case, military members who operate at high altitudes, in their chamber and suck the air out to simulate being at twenty-five thousand feet, or more. The purpose is to allow a person to identify what their hypoxia symptoms are so they can recognize them sooner and correct for equipment failure as soon as possible to avoid incapacitation or death. One of the symptoms is belligerence, which neither she nor anyone at her unit had ever seen until I showed up.

Once we had all finished up the basic training at twenty-five thousand feet, the chamber was taken to twenty-eight thousand feet to show the impact of higher elevations on time of useful consciousness (TUC). This demonstration was to be completed by a single individual while the rest of the people in the chamber simply observed. As the new guy at the unit, I was the selected "volunteer." I was given a child's toy to put shapes in the matching holes while off oxygen. As I started to miss the correct match, my teammates in the chamber started harassing me with comments on the mic. They all had their masks up, so I couldn't see who was talking, but I was getting more pissed with each heckle. I started threatening to beat up or kill everyone, which only caused everyone to laugh harder and make more comments. About this time, I had run out of my TUC and passed out. The other inside observer put my oxygen mask up and I slowly came back awake.

Apparently, everyone at the Aerospace Physiology Unit was excited! It turned out that my hypoxia symptom of belligerence was the first one they had a chance to observe directly, and they happily recorded it for training purposes. The entire unit, including Rachel, quite enjoyed my example—it became a story she shared in all of her training briefs and was what she remembered about me.

What a big relief for me.

☆☆☆

When we first started dating, Rachel was living in Ohio. She was between jobs, struggling to make mortgage payments, and she didn't have a car. I was so committed to this new relationship that I made the decision to change my living arrangements to provide help to her and her boys. I moved all of my belongings from the apartment into storage and started sleeping in the cages once again at work. The money I saved, I sent to her.

I lived in gear cages and barracks next to young SEAL trainees as I trained the new generation of SEALs.

I liked being an instructor, but now at the age of forty-seven, I didn't like living like an FNG again. Eventually I got sick of the cages. I moved students out of one of their rooms on the second floor and disabled the lock, jury-rigging it so only I had access. Finally, I had privacy. Well, I had some privacy. I can't say the same for the three BUD/S students that shared the bathroom with me. They would stay up all night prepping for inspection the next day, cleaning out the bathroom to near perfection, and take off for the workday. I would wake up shortly after and prep myself for the day, showering and brushing my teeth in such a pristine bathroom. Then it was off to inspect the new guys, including this same bathroom. When I got to their room and walked in on their bathroom, I would ream them for the hair and water all over the sink. The amount of restraint they had to not call me out for being the cause of their pain was commendable.

Having nowhere permanent to live, and soon to be retired from SEAL life, I was dedicated to making sure my best chance at happiness was well taken care of. I offered to drive out to Ohio with the BMW X5 I had just bought (with California plates and tinted windows, fully loaded).

I drove for two straight days on the way to Ohio—all day, all night, all day, all night, stopping off only for Red Bull and gasoline.

At the end of my trip, I was on I-275 outside of Cincinnati, Ohio, and nearing my exit to I-75—almost to Rachel—

when I saw six or more police cars on the side of the road. Thinking nothing of it, I passed them. I'd barely gone a couple hundred feet when they all peeled out to surround me, cutting off all three lanes of traffic. I looked in the mirror to find all traffic was stopped about one hundred yards behind me. I had a police car in front of me, one behind me, and another to the left side of me. They forced me onto the side of the road and started questioning me; my foreign accent was not helping. I was so confused—the officers had stopped traffic completely and lights were flashing everywhere. This was way more than a routine traffic stop. They told me that I was following a small red car recklessly close. I didn't remember seeing any red car.

As I handed over my documents, the police officer in my window noticed my military ID. After some questioning, we discovered that we'd both been in Iraq around the same time, and on the same base (while I was raiding Iraqi terrorists, he was training Iraqi police). He returned from his patrol car and told me not to worry about it, then he explained why they had pulled me over. As it turned out, I-75 was a drug-trafficking superhighway, and they thought I was a runner (or a user, or both) because they'd been tracking me on my drive for the last couple of days. I'd been driving nonstop like a madman! We talked for a while, laughed about it, and then I was back on the road to Rachel.

When I arrived at Rachel's house, she was hard at work painting the walls to get it ready to go on the market. She was getting ready to move and needed to spruce things up for buyers, she said, which was a bewildering concept to me. She had to take her kids to school, and like a gentleman I offered to take over the paint job, ignoring the fact that I was cold (Ohio weather is a bit different than California's) and hadn't slept in two nights. It was just some paint—how hard could it be?

Sitting on the ladder in the warm, quiet space, I was trying to paint the wall when I suddenly felt sleepy. The next thing I knew, I woke up passed out on Rachel's living room floor, bright yellow paint spilled everywhere. My first thought was: *Rachel is going to kill me.* I panicked and rushed to the store to buy cleaning supplies, except I had no idea what I needed to clean carpet with and bought what I thought was sure to do the trick in cleaning up the mess: steel wool, paint thinner—anything and everything that would help fix this disaster.

In my genuine, heartfelt effort to clean everything, I ended up leaving spots of paint on her white California Berber carpet, white leather sofa, and a few other belongings. But after some strategic pillow placements and shifting of furniture, I figured I'd done a decent job of hiding the evidence. And I had! I got away with my crime for quite a few months—until we finally managed to sell the house (the market had been gutted by the recession). Unfortunately for me, Rachel—who is a very clever person—noticed things as we packed up the house, like the ruined carpet in the corner, the big splash of yellow across the back of the sofa, and the splotches all over the back of a black side table.

She was horrified, but I told her the whole story and she forgave me. She even told me recently, "I'm just glad you landed on soft, squishy carpet and not hard ceramic tile like they were painting over in the foyer!"

Thank goodness.

Even as my personal life began to fall into place, I struggled to wrap my head around the fact that I would soon be leaving the Navy SEALs forever. I began looking for jobs, trying to think of what career could possibly satisfy me after years in the Teams.

The problem with SEAL life is that it's harder to get out of than it is to get in. I know that sounds impossible given everything you've read, but you must understand how much of your life the Teams occupy and for how long. For years, your SEAL teammates are everything to you: your family, your friends, your coworkers. You eat, sleep, breathe, and fight with them day in and day out. No one in the world knows you better than those guys do. Not only that, but they also understand what you've been through better than anyone ever will.

Rachel helped a lot with this process. When I was put on terminal leave, she helped me do everything from typing up my résumé to teaching me how to negotiate job offers. "Never accept the first one they give you," she said. Rachel helped me post my résumé online for my job search, and three days later I received a call from a software development firm. They asked me some basic screening questions and then invited me to come in for an interview. On my way out, Rachel reiterated: "Do not accept the first offer they give you!" She emphasized for me to come home, we would talk about it, and then I could negotiate for terms I wanted.

Naturally, I said yes to the first offer they gave me. But I promised her that I would listen to her more closely from then on out.

CHAPTER EIGHTEEN

TURBULENCE UPON REENTRY

RACHEL AND I STILL LOVE to reminisce about our dating days. While thinking of stories for this memoir, she brought up an incident that she loves to embarrass me with. She tells it to everyone she meets:

"Thomas was always trying to impress me when we started dating, always trying to be like a knight in shining armor for me. And sometimes his adrenaline really gets the best of him. One day, I went out into the backyard to do some gardening. We had sliding glass doors off the sunroom that led to the backyard. I'd closed the screen door behind me, but not the glass, and as I was watering my flowers, I tugged the hose a bit too hard and the hose's holding box tipped over right onto my foot! And if you've been around those things, especially when most of the hose is still wound up in it, you know they are really heavy. So, I made this little sound, like, 'ouch!' And Thomas came barreling out of the house like I'd screamed Bloody Mary or something. He cleared the steps from the door to the patio in a single step and pivoted quickly around the corner, and with great concern asked me if I was okay. When I looked up from my slightly sore, but not maimed toe, I saw him looking at me with such great concern *through* my screen door. Yes! My screen door that he was holding in front of him with both hands. I started laughing so hard, I was crying. He asked me what was so funny and I just shook my head. It was not until he knew I was okay that he took a moment to review the situation and see that he was still holding my screen door. He ever so sweetly said, 'Oh, sorry. I will put this back.' It was the funniest thing ever!"

In my own defense, I didn't even know the screen door was there! Of course, that wasn't the only time I embarrassed myself in front of Rachel in my attempts to woo her.

During a visit to the Newport Aquarium with Rachel and her kids, we decided to get some ice cream, which was kept by the cash register in the café in an old-school freezer. I approached the freezer—and the teenager running the register—and grabbed the lid's handle. I firmly lifted the lid to grab ice creams for the kids and tore the whole lid clean off the tracks. These were actually sliding doors meant to be slid from right side to left side, and not hinged doors for lifting up. Oops! Rachel was immediately laughing out loud, while the cashier just stared at me like I was Godzilla or something come to destroy his workplace! I heard my two little kids whispering behind me: "How did he do that? He ripped the freezer doors." I think I muttered, "Sorry," trying to place the lid back on the freezer like before, but it was no use.

It wasn't always sunshine and roses while we were dating. I think it's important to highlight how difficult it can be for members of the military to leave the service and return to civilian life. Rachel and I fought a lot early on in our relationship as she worked to domesticate me. I have to admit that I am now fully domesticated, thanks to Rachel. I'm grateful to her now, and deep down I think I was at the time, too, but I know she had a lot of moments of pulling her hair out. She would often have to remind me that I could not carry on in civil society without a filter; I had to just be Thomas again. So, Drago had been fired and put in the "cage." No more Drago. And after spending so long being Drago, Thomas felt like a complete stranger to me.

You see, coming home from war is a lot more than stepping off a plane and onto American soil. Much like entering the military, leaving it is a process, and it takes hard work, time, and patience. This is especially true of the Navy SEALs, in my experience. Some guys can't live without the Teams. Others hack it back in the civilian world for a while but eventually find ways to come back to the Teams or similar jobs in the contracting world. With our high operations tempo and combat deployments, sitting at a computer to complete training or working on distance learning was not an option for many of us. This made transitioning into the civilian work world more challenging. The military provides structure, camaraderie, and stability to a lot of people who have never experienced any of those things before, and it can be extremely difficult to leave behind.

In combat, I did not see anything that the Navy didn't prepare me to see. I did not do anything the Navy didn't prepare me to do. I don't have any regrets from my actions in the war. There is nothing that ever bothered me about the war. On the other hand, traumatic brain injury (TBI) is a different story. As an NSW Lead Breacher, I was exposed to countless close proximity explosions; some of them caused bleeding from my nose or ears. It definitely had some effect on my health, and I did have trouble sleeping as I transitioned to civilian life. I'd wake up in the middle of the night every night, wide awake at 2:00 or 3:00 a.m. In the past, when talking to my fellow SEALs about it, the consensus was "ghosts." But the more information that began to come through about these problems, the more I began to realize that the damage done during my time in the military was still with me. Every breach, explosion, shock wave, and concrete powder inhalation had left us with varying degrees of physical trauma. This has affected things like my memory, my balance, and my speech.

I carried a lot of bad habits from my time as a SEAL for quite a while. Probably some bad habits from my earlier life, too, now that I think about it. Rachel—who has always been significantly more proper than me—had to tell me on multiple occasions not to just spit out the first thought that came to my head when someone said something stupid or not to beat up some random guy on the street just because I thought he looked at me funny. Sometimes I felt like I was taking etiquette classes.

But Rachel also told me at multiple points during our early relationship how much she was learning from me, too. She said, "I'm amazed at how you're always thinking in black and white. If you have to make a decision, you make it, without hesitation. I always get stuck in the gray areas, and while nuance is a good thing, too much can lead to indecision. I like how you're able to commit to a decision once you've made it."

She understood that as a SEAL, my life often came down to split-second decisions. I had to make them a lot, too—in the moment, as the situation was unfolding. There was no time for hemming and hawing. But we learned from each other in that respect. I came to understand that not *every* decision in civilian life warrants (or deserves) a black-or-white answer; she came to learn how to be a better, more confident decision-maker. One of the keys to our relationship that we established during this time was learning to respect each other's views while leaving room to learn new information and approaches from each other.

My BUD/S students also shared how much they valued my perspective and what they learned from me. At the end of each phase, students were required to write a review of the phase and provide evaluations for all the instructors. One of my students commented, "Instructor Drago was so motivating. I can't imagine how much more motivated I would be if I understood half of what he said." Other students may not have found my insight as motivating, especially during pool comp. The most significant test for the second phase was the pool competency test. This required the student to perform emergency procedures exactly by regulations while properly managing their air. This evaluation was done at the bottom of pool with their open-circuit scuba. This had to be passed before they could move onto the LAR-5 rebreather. The instructor would introduce a problem the student had to solve without any deviation from the established procedures, rules, and regulations. The test is so strict that even if the student successfully completed the recovery steps by regulation, if they gave the thumbs up with the wrong hand, it meant failure for the student. Students who did not manage their air properly would sometimes pass out and had to be taken to the surface and out of the pool by the instructor where medical staff attended to the student. They had to prove they could maintain consciousness with proper air management while solving a difficult task as presented by the instructor. You can imagine my chagrin when one of my students who passed out after being unsuccessful in solving the problem came to, looked up at me, and said, "Instructor Drago, did I pass? It was very hard and I didn't give up."

"You must be kidding me. In my opinion, you were napping on the job! How can I pass you? The entire class was looking at you while you were sleeping by the pool, and we had a hard time waking you up. That was demotivating to the class, and you fail!" Of course, I would debrief the student and provide detailed instructions on why he failed and what he needed to improve.

Students passing out during this evolution was not common, but it did happen on occasion. Student safety was paramount in every phase and every evolution of training. As with any failure, the instructor would take the time to go over in detail what the student did wrong and why they failed, and what they needed to improve if they hoped to pass the next time.

There was no way I was letting Rachel get away. I was committed and wanted to lock in her commitment, so I decided I was going to ask her to marry me. I bought books on the diamond requirements: the best color, clarity, etc. As an enlisted guy, I didn't have a lot of money and went to the local military exchange retail store on North Island to make sure I maximized my dollars. They showed me a variety of options and I decided on high-quality beauty, like my lady. The next part was figuring out how to ask her. I didn't have enough money for a fancy restaurant or extravagant excursion. So, I went with what I knew best, the shooting range and surrounded with support from my fellow SEALs.

Fortunately, when I told Rachel we would be spending the day shooting at Niland, she was actually very excited. She had no idea what was really planned. One of the best gifts Rachel continues to give me is patience, and thankfully, she had a lot of patience while sitting alone in the common area at the Niland SEAL compound for over an hour while the guys and I prepped the line. I left her sitting there with no television, no phone signal, and only some outdated gun magazines.

When everything was all set, I went back to the lounge and was happy to find her still upbeat for the day, and I took her outside to the range. I introduced her to my teammates and had one of my friends film it all. We started with the M4 and a full magazine, standing up. She was a good shot, and my heart skipped a beat. I was already in love, and this was the icing on the cake. I had the same routine for each gun. She fired all the guns in our inventory and did it very well.

The last gun was set up on the ground, and was the Mk 48 light machine gun, the most important gun of all. Her task was to load the gun by opening the tray, loading the belt ammunition, and shutting the tray down, taking it off safe, and shooting. What had taken so long was figuring out how to hide the ring in a way that kept the surprise but didn't damage the ring, and how to hide my note in the tray. I got down on my knee next to her as she opened the tray, which popped up, and there was the diamond ring hanging from it with a note: "marry me."

She was surprised! I was relieved and I took her hands in mine and asked her if she would be my wife.

She said, "Yes!"

Rachel and I were married on August 18, 2007. That also happens to be the date of the Battle of Thermopylae in 480 BC, and we were married in a small town that was named after the Spartan king Leonidas. I had been fascinated by ancient Greek and Roman history for years, and these coincidences felt like a confirmation of our beautiful life ahead. We have five children together, including three from our previous marriages: our older boys are in their twenties—Adam is happily married and has a young daughter; Blake is starting college after serving honorably as a US Marine with deployments to Afghanistan; and Connor is loving life while serving in the US Coast Guard. Our two little teenagers from our marriage are Grace, the little lady of the house, and Dorian, our future warrior.

☆ ☆ ☆

I officially retired from the U.S. Navy SEALs at the rank of Petty Officer First Class on June 31, 2011. I am proud of the contributions I made to the Teams, and thankful for the great men I was able to serve with and learn from. The following are excerpts from my BUPERS 1610-1 (Evaluation Report & Counseling Record) covering my combat deployments:

- IT2 Dzieran is an impressive SEAL whose recent achievements in OIF have brought significant credit to himself and NSW [Naval Special Warfare] community.

- Participated in ## combat missions including ## Direct Action missions.
- Lead Breacher for ## combat operations, and conducted ## explosive breaches. Relying on his technical expertise, coalition forces captured high value targets and prevented injury to non-combatants in close proximity to explosives.
- IT2 Dzieran is a Mission-Focused SEAL who volunteered for a second back-to-back deployment to Iraq.
- Conducted ## Combined and Joint Direct Action and Special Reconnaissance missions which eliminated significant Anti-Coalition Forces.
- EXPERT BREACHER. Developed innovative breaching techniques […]. Outstanding results with zero non-combatant casualties.
- AMBASSADOR. Planned, Coordinated, and Led a Personal Security Detail for the Polish Prime Minister visit to Iraq.
- Consummate SEAL and Warrior – Committed to Serving. 100% mission success executing ## combat missions!
- Dzieran is a proven warrior whose outstanding performance during sustained combat operation in support of Operation Iraqi Freedom cannot be overstated.
- COMBAT LEADER. Lead breacher during ## Direct Action missions in Iraq resulting in capture […] insurgents, numerous weapon caches, and sensitive intelligence. Masterfully employed ## explosive and mechanical breaches.
- Trained, supervised, and led all NSW Breachers deployed to Iraq from April–July 2005.
- TACTICAL EXPERT. Through adept and skilled observation, he personally prevented ## non-combatant casu-

alties by intervening and replacing ## explosive breaching charges.
- Displayed poise despite prolonged combat exposure.
- Dzieran's contribution to the Global War on Terrorism cannot be overstated.

★ EPILOGUE ★

I HAD A LOT OF learning to do when I first arrived in America. There was the time I went to a grocery store and saw some guys outside drinking from bottles in paper bags. One of them saw me and told me to give them a quarter; I told him he should give *me* a quarter, and without another word, I smacked him upside the head. That's something I wouldn't do today—even now I'm amazed that I got away with something like that and didn't get shot.

America has a steep learning curve. Coming from Communist Poland, I was completely dumbfounded by all the things Americans did that were different from what I'd known my whole life. In America, I learned that if people get into a fight, you call the police to intervene; growing up in Poland, you had to handle your business yourself. If the police became involved, they would only escalate the situation. We were surrounded by a violent political regime, and the memory of World War II was very present and intense. Polish people were hungry; they weren't interested in being friendly or giving anyone the benefit of the doubt. In a constant state of distrust, misinformation, and fear, violence in all its forms becomes the norm.

But that's not to say I don't miss Poland. I do. It may seem hard to believe, but I really do miss it sometimes.

Sometimes I miss Polish food, the taste and memories that come with it, especially the food that I grew up with that my mother made. We didn't have a lot to eat, so every time my mother made something special, like ham on Christmas, it stuck with me. To this day, I can remember the taste and smell and texture of it. I miss the streets of Poland; they had a certain atmosphere, a certain character, which is very different from anywhere I've been in America.

Even the air! In America the air is so clean, I find myself at times missing the smell of smoke and gasoline. Spending time on my grandfather's farm while I was growing up, I had to load stacks of hay onto carts and tie them together; I hated the smell of it when I was a kid, but I'm nostalgic for it now.

Indeed, I have a lot of nostalgia for parts of my young life. In America, people like to smile and say hi; as a kid growing up in Poland, it was very different. If you looked too long at someone, they'd get defensive and snap at you, "What are you looking at?" Everyone was always going about their business. I don't miss that, but there's a part of me that is nostalgic for what I used to know. The tension of people always being ready to fight was a brutal but very real part of my life and the lives of many others.

There was joy, too, growing up. There was always singing and vodka with family; my aunts and uncles were very close to us physically and emotionally, and I miss the feeling of being with them, laughing and eating and drinking, us kids stealing vodka under the table. The little things were so valuable and meant so much, even things that may seem simple and silly to others. I remember with a smile on my face the Christmas I received a pencil sharpener as a gift from my mom. She had saved up her money for this gift and knew how important it was to me; as a young avid artist I was so happy to have my very own sharpener—it was all mine.

Reflecting on memories from Poland...it was a hard life, but now, I mostly try to remember the good things. The Soviet Union collapsed between 1991–1992 and with it, the entire Socialist ideology. With the new, freely elected Polish government, I was fully exonerated along with the other political prisoners.

I have been able to go back to a Poland a few times since I left.

My first visit back to Poland after moving to America was with my SEAL platoon during my first deployment as a Navy SEAL in 1995. We went there to train with Polish special forces. When I'd stepped onto the plane leaving Poland back in 1983, I thought I'd never be able to come back. I'd left the country a felon and a political target; I came back to visit as a respected American citizen.

In 1995, not a lot had changed since I left, though. Things seemed very normal from my perspective. My teammates and I went to a restaurant and the staff promptly started yelling at us; the guys were saying we should go somewhere else, and I had to tell them that this behavior was normal and that this was the best restaurant around.

I certainly never thought the Communist regime in Eastern Europe would collapse. My old friend from Hrubieszów prison, Edward Kędziorski, and I reconnected during this trip. He gave me some memorabilia and together we reminisced about our time spent in prison. I was so relieved to see him again and liked to hear about his life after getting out.

When I visited Poland in 2009, it was a totally different world from the one I'd grown up in. All the villages

I remembered had been cleaned, painted, and paved. The kids were well fed, and the parents looked happy. I appeared on Polish TV during that visit, and I mentioned how surprised I was to see people smiling, saying hello, being generous with each other. It was unlike any Poland I'd ever seen before.

Every time I return to Poland, I see more and more changes. It's more like America now than ever, and it astounds me every time I see it. If a Polish person today were to behave like I used to behave, beating people up and misbehaving, they would be outright shunned. Poland does have problems with organized crime as we do in America, but like America, they deal with it in their own way.

Rachel never saw the old gray Poland—that chapter of terror and Socialism is now closed in Polish history. We stayed in Old Warsaw, which is functionally a museum now. It was impactful, seeing everything rebuilt and learning the history of the Warsaw Uprising.

On our first visit to Poland together, we went to see my father. It was the first time that I had seen him or even spoken with him since I was fifteen years old. It was a little awkward at first, but soon we fell into good conversation, catching up after years of being estranged.

There's a sense of deep pride and belonging among Poles. Throughout the country, there are memorials and monuments to victims of the Communist regime and their atrocities everywhere you look. But the people have always been resilient, and they are fiercely patriotic and protective of their hard-earned freedom. To this day, Polish people are so proud of what they've accomplished in the wake of the collapse of the USSR. For my part, the power of being there, seeing the bricks taken from the rubble I once played in being used as foundations for new structures, was incredible.

I love Poland, and I still get asked sometimes if I would ever move back. And every time I say no: I'm an American now. I am an American by choice. I'm fiercely proud of my roots, but America is where my heart belongs, where I live, and America is where I'll die.

I'm so happy to have made so many positive new memories of Poland with Rachel and our family. I'm happy to have so many memories from my life after the SEALs, period. Too many of my teammates have struggled after leaving the Teams. It is hard to get into SEAL Teams, many fail; it is hard to leave SEAL Teams, many fail. The fact that I'd met Rachel, and that she'd put up with me in the earliest days of our relationship, put me on the path of a new and far more promising future. I have been fully domesticated by Rachel.

I'll always remember after we first met, that same week she came to visit me from Ohio, I decided I had to do everything I could to woo her. All I really did was embarrass myself, but it makes for a great story in hindsight. I'd pulled out all the stops (or as many as I could afford) for the week she was in town: motorcycle rides, movie dates, walks on the beach, you name it. One evening, we'd taken my Jeep to a dance club in town.

Why I decided to take the woman of my dreams to a dance club, I have no idea. It wasn't that I thought she wouldn't like it—I knew she would! But she didn't know that I couldn't dance to save my life. I had to brave it in my efforts to impress her, and upon the advice of friends, I took her to the most crowded place where I could hide my lack of dance expertise. When I say I was a terrible dancer, I mean it. I could not dance if my life depended on it. Knowing how it would go, instead of dancing, I opted to clear the dance floor for my lady so she had room to dance and ensured no one was within four feet of her, all around. If someone started to get close, I would push them away and ensure they knew they were not welcome. There were a few who gave me dirty looks, but I was a pretty big guy at the time, so no one messed with us. She smiled at me and appeared to be very happy.

Until we got back to the parking garage. As soon as we approached the Jeep and I saw the headlights were barely on, I knew I was in trouble.

In my nervousness, I had accidentally left the lights on the whole time we were out. By the time we'd gotten back, the battery had been completely drained and we were stranded. I didn't feel very smart.

I attempted to flag down help, but was unintentionally scaring off passersby who sped up when they saw me approaching their car. This was going nowhere, so I left Rachel in the Jeep and took off to a lower level of the parking garage in hopes of finding a security guard who might be able to help. While I was away, Rachel was able to flag down quite a few cars wanting to provide aid for a beautiful lady and her distressed vehicle. I was unsuccessful in finding assistance but came back to the Jeep to find a smug, very triumphant Rachel sitting in the driver seat of my Jeep pushing on the gas to ensure the juice from the other car giving the jump was going to get the battery going for the ride home. I thought it would be quite awkward heading home, but Rachel made me feel at ease and even joked about the situation.

Rachel stuck around. Even though I still can't dance.

For as long as I can remember, America has represented so many good things: freedom, prosperity, and the opportunity to become exactly who you want to be and are able to be in life. These weren't part of my life growing up. No one in Communist-controlled countries really ever had any of those things; some may have thought they did, but there was always a catch, some law or loophole that prohibited them from being truly free. The way I understood it growing up, America was where you went to be just that: truly free.

When I came to America, my chief goal was to be independent. My original dream was to buy an old used U-Haul, cut some windows out of the hauler, and make it my own little "mobile home." It would be mine, and to me, this would be the epitome of making it in America. While I obviously never did end up doing that, it feels like the perfect encapsulation of my early American dream.

Because even as my dream changed shape over the years, I was living somewhere where such change was encouraged. At their core, Americans are proud, generous, and loving people. They are quick to aid old friends and newcomers alike. Regardless of where you go in this great country, you will find good people, just like I did, and they will show you why America is so admired around the world.

This country made me a better person, too. As you've read, I have my own history of being less than perfect. I used to think everyone was out for themselves, that I had to be ready to hit someone before they could hit me. I knew hunger and cold, and how cruel a government built on lies could be. And then I came to America, where strangers gave me food to eat and put money in my pockets and got me on my feet. Strangers! But I wasn't all that surprised. And those first gestures have stayed with me my entire life in America, reminding me even when things are hard that there are good people in this country. People who are doing their best to do right by themselves, their families, and their neighbors. Good people, trying to do one good thing after another.

Some may say America is not perfect, but I disagree. There is a reason America is known as the beacon of freedom for the entire world. Like everything in life, there is good and bad, and I believe it is our responsibility as Americans to learn our history as both. In order to fully appreciate what we have now, we have to understand where we've been, how we got here, and how we keep what we have. Freedom is not free; it must be treasured, and it must be protected at all costs.

American history nowadays is a complicated subject, and one I am still learning plenty about. But I would rather we confront our shared American past and use that knowledge to create a better future for ourselves. It's shockingly easy to backslide into authoritarianism and censorship. The suppression of information is just one of the many warning signs.

As uncomfortable as it may be to have conversations with people we disagree with, I think it's important to do—it's how I learned and continue to learn about America and what it represents. Lies and corruption can affect anyone and can convince people to do the worst things.

(And when those people work in government, things can get really scary.) The unilateral stripping of rights and mistreatment of people based on who they are or what they believe in are not the actions of a healthy republic. I sometimes have to remind people around me to not take their freedom for granted. That it can be taken from them at a moment's notice.

I have seen what happens when a totalitarian government takes control, and it's why I am so grateful to be a proud American citizen. America is my country and I consider myself blessed to live here. This was where I found the SEALs, who gave me a new life and a new sense of purpose. Where else but America can you show up with only a bag of clothes, barely able to speak English, and rise to the ranks of the world's greatest fighting force? America is where I found love, a renewed sense of faith, and was able to build a family and a life for them without ever again having to look over my shoulder.

I think more of us need to appreciate how much America offers. So many people don't realize how lucky they are to be able to say whatever they want without looking over their shoulder with the fear of government retaliation. While other consequences may result, I have never had to worry about the things I've said landing me in prison while in America. In former Communist Poland? Well, you've seen what my experiences were like there.

It is important to also engage in conversations with others to understand what it is they are trying to say, why they are saying it, and what their point is (if any). Assuming that you know what they mean, becoming upset, and wanting to censor them is not the answer. Trust me, I know all too well what it's like to say something innocent but my accent or word choice gets me in trouble. The English language continues to challenge me to this day. If you haven't figured it out by now, I love sweets. One day, only a few years ago, I was asking my wife if she could make dessert for me, but my pronunciation almost got me "fired" from my "domesticated" husband position. I told Rachel, "You know what, I really want to eat kimberly." She looked at me with huge eyes and asked me, "What did you say?"

"Kimberly. I really love kimberly and want to eat kimberly."

"*Who* is Kimberly?"

"What?" I was confused. "I just want to eat kimberly, what do you mean who?"

She paused for a few moments, took a deep breath, and asked, "What do you mean by Kimberly?"

"You know that dessert we usually get at the restaurants. It's my favorite and I really want to eat it. Can you make it?"

She relaxed instantly and started laughing… "Crème brûlée."

"Yes, that! That is what I want." I wasn't fired and Rachel made me a truly tasty crème brûlée.

The English language is still a work in progress for me. As my youngest son pointed out recently when discussing my attempt to claim I now speak English *fluently*, "Yes Dad, you are able to put two sentences together easily, and you might even be able to get a paragraph together at times. Is that considered *fluent*?"

Ultimately, I believe the American Dream is about more than material prosperity; it's about being able to live a safe, simple, fulfilling life and having the freedom and opportunity to pursue our individual dreams, regardless of what you think or how you vote. Patriotism, to me, means respecting one's neighbor and loving one's family and being willing to defend both. I fought against a totalitarian government when I was younger. Doing so taught me to be strong and to never lose sight of what it is I'm defending. Whether it's a person, or a flag, or a place, every American can love something about this country and fight to make it a better home for everyone. For me, at the end of the day, I owe everything to this country, and the people in it, and I wouldn't have it any other way.

I have my own reasons for how I feel about America. You might have others, or you might not feel the way I do at all. And that's okay. My goal with this book was to tell the story of my life before coming to America, and what happened after. There's a good chance my own children will learn new things about me when they read this book; as their parents, Rachel and I shield them from a lot of my early life. Even our eldest son has learned more from listening to my interviews on podcasts than from me directly. You might also disagree with this approach, but at the end of the day, I simply want my children to be shaped by *their* present as they grow up, not influenced by *my* past.

It's all we can do as parents to set a good example for our children. My goal, as it has been since the day I came to this country, is to simply be a better American tomorrow than I am today—or was yesterday. This is my *Pledge to America.*

THE SPIRIT OF THE POLISH PEOPLE AND SOLIDARITY LEADERSHIP

BEING LOCKED UP WAS TOUGH, and yet it helped me grow in my understanding of the complexity of the situation in Poland. There were great men in prison with me, Solidarity leaders who inspired me with their strength and relentless courage in the face of evil.

Forty years after my imprisonment, in October 2022, I was able to reconnect with former political prisoners in person at Hrubieszów. It was surreal to meet with those whom I had been imprisoned with: former Solidarity members and others who opposed Socialist ideology. We shared stories of our lives since imprisonment, as well as reflected on our time in prison and the effects of martial law in 1981. We were provided a tour of the very same prison we spent time in as political prisoners. I stood in the exact same prison cell that I had been locked up in, and I even walked the same yard as a free man with the same men I once walked with as a political prisoner. When I was imprisoned at Hrubieszów in the '80s, I was branded a criminal; however, on my return I was treated as a hero. I am grateful to have permission to share the following stories of my friends in hopes that you will have a better appreciation for the environment as we lived through it.

KRZYSZTOF BIŃKOWSKI

This unusual—and from today's point of view, fascinating—atmosphere of the first hours and days of December 1981 is contained in the memoirs of Krzysztof Bińkowski— arrested, longtime activist of the opposition and Solidarity trade union from the city of Radom. Krzysztof and other activists were leading figures in resistance and the fight against Communism in Poland. Later, even after his arrest, Krzysztof continued the fight for human rights and status of political prisoner.

Here are fragments of his journal that he wrote during the struggle to free Poland from the yoke of Communism and Socialism. Excerpts from Krzysztof Bińkowski's journal with his permission:

> *December 13, 1981*
> It's ten o'clock in the morning. I overslept. […] I turn on the radio. Soon there will be radio segment "60 Minutes Per Hour" with Fedorowicz and Kaczmarek. Silence in the speakers. Suddenly, the door opens. My mother rushes into the house. She was at the

market by the bus station to buy a piece of meat for dinner.

"War!" she says in a shaky voice. Police are rounding up and arresting people in the city, they are breaking up "Solidarity"!!!

Cold sweat doused me. I had barely heard the news when there was a banging on the door. We stopped the conversation and didn't speak for a long time. After some time, the banging on the door stopped. I hurriedly buried the more important things and dressed warmly— just in case. After some time, the banging on the door was repeated.

December 14, 1981
It was already about nine o'clock when I entered the room of the factory director, Mr. Foremniak. Then the so-called "People's Commissar" offered for me to sign a "declaration of loyalty" to the military junta who just imposed the martial law. I laughed at him and called him names, and compared the military junta to the Chile and El Salvador regimes, etc. Some of these phrases, such as comparing them to the dictators of El Salvador and Chile, have found their way into the courtroom in prosecutorial charges. Olszewski called the Police Headquarters to bring the car and transport me to the police station. [...]

I was informed by a state security police officer that I was being detained. I was handcuffed with other Polish patriots and we were all transported to prison. The Communists arrested our books too!

December 18, 1981
Handcuffed to the seat of a police car, I was rushed towards the city of Radom. The thick snow was pouring the whole time, frosting the car's windows. We were passed by a line of police cars, driving with emergency lights and sirens on to create an atmosphere of terror and fear. [...]

February 11, 1982
We have been joined by several more political prisoners. [...]. That day we learned that before our arrival at the prison in the city of Łęczyca, a lot of leaflets were thrown from behind the prison wall. We were called again for negotiations. Referring to the Charter of Human and Citizen Rights signed by the People's Republic of Poland, we requested the status of "political prisoner." The answer to our demands was a broadcast by prison radio. In the broadcast it was said that the leaders of the "Solidarity" movement committed treason against the Socialist state. [...]

May 1982
May began, and news of demonstrations and clashes with special police units began to

arrive from outside the prison walls. On May 1, 1982, a "Black March" took place in the city of Łódź along Piotrkowska Street. These protests were attended by more than fifty thousand people. Fights with the police broke out in the cities of Nowa Huta, Warsaw, Lublin, Gdańsk, Poznań, Wrocław, and dozens of others. These protests lasted until mid-May. [...]

June 5, 1982
After arriving to prison in the city of Hrubieszów, prison guards attempted to make us conform to prison regulations. Therefore, from the beginning we started to break their rules. It started with us winning two hours of being able to lay on the bed in the afternoon. Of course, penalties were dished out by prison guards along with our win. Obviously, this accelerated work on the first version of our own set of rules, with which we were replacing the prison rules and regulations.

We established that when called to the prison warden office, at the entrance to the room we would only say "good morning" and mention our name. However, we omitted all the additional formalities required by prison regulations (e.g., This is prisoner so-and-so asking for permission to enter the office).

June 21, 1982
I have just been called to the warden's office to be punished for lying on the bed in the after-

noon. I walked in, said good morning, and stated my name. That's all I said and waited. "Get out!" shouted the warden. So, I went out into the hallway, and after a short moment I moved towards my cell. The prison guard came after me and brought me back into the warden's office. Again, I did not announce myself according to the prison regulations: "Mister warden! Convicted so-and-so, the son of such-and-such reports his entry to receive punishment." At the end of the "visit," another formula is expected: "Mister warden, convicted so-and-so asks for permission to leave." These phrases are to emphasize the total dependence of the prisoner, that he must ask for everything. I refused to conform and say any of these required phrases. The prison warden kept calling me back and throwing me out of the office multiple times. I didn't conform. The warden got tired and gave me ten days of isolation.

[...]

In the fight for the status of political prisoner, in the first stage we established the following rules:

1. For beating a political prisoner – four days of hunger strike.

2. For solitary confinement and "hard bed" – three days of hunger strike.

3. For other form of punishments – two days of hunger strike.

If the punishment was suspended, we suspended our hunger strike.

ANDRZEJ KRASUSKI

Andrzej Krasuski was an activist of the Solidarity Trade Union, the first organization in Warsaw Pact countries totally independent from the Communist Party. When arrested by the Communists for organizing protests against martial law in Poland, instead of defending himself, he started schooling Communist judges and prosecutors about the dignity, patriotism, and dangers of Communist ideology. A fragment of his defense, or rather his statement about the tyranny of Communism and legality of martial law, is shared here with Andrzej Krasuski's permission:

> Hearing before the Provincial Court on July 28, 1982, in the case of "Solidarity" from the city of Bełchatów:
>
> "*Court* – What does the defendant have to say in the case?
>
> *Andrzej Krasuski* – At the outset, I would like to confirm what I said at the end of the investigation. First of all, I do not admit my guilt. I believe that what I did cannot be considered in terms of guilt at all. On the other hand, I admit to committing some of the acts accused of me. From March to mid-April, I cooperated with the bulletin "Solidarność Wojenna" [Wartime Solidarity] from No. 6 and 7. I also distributed to several colleagues

from work our newsletters and publications that I received in Warsaw. I also admit that I handed over [...] a printer and a container with paint. I made the printing device myself on the construction site in October. The Workers' Committee of The Geoproject, of which I was a member, entrusted me in September 1981 with editing and reproduction of the company bulletin, hence the need to make a printing house, which then remained in my possession until March 1982. [...] There is no evidence of me being at the meetings after December 13. In order to anticipate any questions, I declare that out of the group of defendants I know only three people: Wyczachowski, Mr. Matyśkiewicz from cooperation related to the newsletter, and Mr. Gajderowicz from social contacts— we live close to each other, and we know each other from the action to help the families of those imprisoned. Col. Gajderowicz walked around the apartments of the internees' families with me in order to get an idea of the needs of these people. In addition, I do not agree with the wording of the accusation regarding the quality of the information we disseminate and the vague assumption about the possibility of causing riots or social anxiety in the city of Bełchatów. I believed and still believe that our information was true, and as for the possibility of causing civil unrest and anxiety, I think that by the act of martial law on December 13, someone else did it for us [the Communist government]. That is all I have to say about the allegations.

I would like to give the court a little more information about the motives of my activity, Your Honor. December 13 found me in Warsaw at my family home. Imposing a martial law was a shock for me and probably for the whole society. From the first day, an unprecedented attack, a deceitful attack, was launched on my Solidarity [Trade] Union. It was one of the most outrageous acts. For example, I will give you a few things that disturbed me the most. [...] Another thing: in a manner as slanderous and primitive, the mass media accused and continue to accuse "Solidarity" of preparing an armed takeover of power. I, as did millions of Poles, wiped my eyes with amazement on December 13. I looked around with friends, and other, sometimes more powerful company organizations, and somehow nowhere could I see those hordes of "Solidarity" thugs who were hungry for blood and murder, who allegedly murdered women and children, according to the earlier prepared lists. I ask—Your Honor—where are these ammunition and weapons depots and in general the entire organizational base, material in the field of armament, which is needed after all for this grand scale takeover, if someone is actually planning a coup? And where are the possible contractors of such work? The answer is simple—nowhere, because this hoax spread by the mass media is a brazen provocation aimed at scaring the public, an apocalyptic vision of a bloody civil war.

[…] For any thinking citizen, the answer is clear. The party and the government needed constant upheavals, protests, and disturbances to be able to condemn an anarchy and finally [under these pretenses] impose the martial law. In general, the very mechanism of introducing martial law was suspicious […]. Since when does the Presidium of the Sejm have the right to suspend the entire Sejm without agreement with the Deputies? And we know that this decision automatically triggered the prerogatives of the Council of State and enabled it to introduce martial law. In addition, the announcement of martial law—without the date and signature—as if it had been printed much earlier and the clients were not sure who in the future will serve as Chairman of the Council of State. Also…

Judge: The accused talks about undoubtedly interesting cases, but the court admonishes the accused to talk about the topic, i.e. about his activity. The defendant's speech is actually a political speech, not an explanation before the court. Please talk about it.

Andrzej Krasuski: Your Honor! I think I'm talking about it. I'm not going to argue here about a pack of leaflets this way or that way. I see my defense mainly in presenting to the court the reasons that guided me as widely as possible.

Judge: The court would like to hear something more about the specific actions of the accused, and not only the justifications for the illegal activities of the "Solidarity" union.

Andrzej Krasuski: I am a member of "Solidarity" and I have connected my personal fate with this organization. In addition, I believe that the question of the legality or illegality of such actions should be approached very carefully. [...] For example, in June 1956, Poznan workers took to the streets illegally and in all the majesty of the law, some of them were killed and some were imprisoned in criminal cases. And yet today, the memory of those times and people is being rehabilitated.

Judge: The court is aware of this. But we are called to apply the law, not to create it. There is a decree on martial law in force and we are applying it today.

Andrzej Krasuski's Attorney (Mr. Siła Nowicki): Were there any reasons that prompted you to be active in the bulletin?

Andrzej Krasuski: Yes. First of all, the need to fight the lie of the mass media. For example, the allegedly binding principle that martial law does not serve retaliation against the members of the Union was advertised. We all know that is not true. In order to not be accused of demagogy, I will give an example—this example is myself. In January, I was fired from my job. The director told me and others that he was doing it at the request of the PZPR [PZPR—Polish Communist Party] Committee. There were many such cases throughout the city of Bełchatów. With all that I said, our bulletin fought. It was for informational purposes only. [...] I take this opportunity to submit a request to the prosecutor to take care of the editorial offices of the *People's Tribune, Workers' Voice* [two leading Communist newspapers], and other mass media. Unlike our activities, the lies that have been proclaimed by these newspapers genuinely provoke social distrust and unrest. Defending my Union [Solidarity] from slander was and is my duty. There are also deeper, more important reasons. As history teaches us, [...] the greatest—apart from biological annihilation—misfortune that can befall a state or a nation is the loss by citizens of the belief that they themselves decide their own fate and the fate of their country, that they can shape their reality themselves. And what do we hear in the official press, radio, and television? This can be put essentially as: "You [Polish people] see, as soon as we [Communists] let go a little, you start anarchy and revolt. Not only that. Even for the leaders you could choose, you chose only CIA agents or secret lovers of Mr. Hupka and Chaya. By the very action of publishing the Bulletin, we wanted to convince people that all is not lost yet and that the Union [Solidarity Trade Union] lives and fights for common causes.

Attorney (Maurer): So, you avoided inciting people to speak. Is that why you have given up further publication of the list of collaborators [Communist collaborators] and is this also the opinion of Mr. Wyczachowski?

Andrzej Krasuski: Of course. We resigned from publishing the list of Communist collaborators because it aroused controversy. I was dismissed from work and no longer had contact with coworkers. [...] For us, a collaborator is anyone who cooperates with Communist authorities of any level in repressing of Solidarity members. There are such people on our lists.

[...]

Judge: The accused will probably agree that such a message, especially in the case of sending [Polish citizens] to the USSR, could cause anxiety?

Andrzej Krasuski: Your Honor! Nowadays, with the existing sharp divisions in society, every piece of information carries the danger of causing anxiety, [...]. So, the most important thing is that the information is simply true.

[...]

Judge. Does the accused think that offensive texts about state and party activists are acceptable if one fights only for the truth and whether such publications do not incite people against the prevailing legal and state order?

Andrzej Krasuski: Humor and laughter are the strongest weapons used for centuries. There is nothing immoral about it.

Judge. Let the accused and those present in the room assess for themselves whether the so-called phrases that I'm about to read are ridiculous at all, or maybe sometimes just offensive:

[...]"

The judge did read aloud some of the poems that were making a mockery of Communist party officials. The reaction was totally opposite from what the judge expected. Constant laughter and quiet cheers could be heard throughout the courtroom. Some people quickly scribbled the poems onto paper and passed them outside. These poems quickly spread like wildfire among Poles.

Krzysztof Bińkowski and Andrzej Krasuski were some of the leading figures in the Solidarity Trade Union in Poland. They led the resistance against Socialist oppression and continued their fight even after being arrested and locked up in prison. Krzysztof and Andrzej, together with thousands of other Polish patriots like Lech Walesa, Jerzy Kaniewski, Witold Kaszuba, Jerzy Kropiwnicki, Edward Kędziorski, Marek Łada, Krzysztof Patora, Zbigniew Rybarkiewicz, and Longin Chlebowski contributed to the fall of Communism and Socialism in Eastern Europe. They started the process, and today the Warsaw Pact no longer exists.

Today, Poland is free from Socialism and Communism. It is economically and politically strong. In fact, Article 13 of Poland's constitution prohibits the existence of political parties or other organizations "whose programs are based upon totalitarian methods and the modes of activity of national Socialism, Fascism and Communism."

The people of Poland are determined that there will never again be prisons in Poland holding people for their views, beliefs, or faith. The real history of Poland is being taught in schools, and the tragedy of Socialism will never again be repeated in Poland.

It was an honor for me to be part of this movement and work together with these brave Poles.

★ ACKNOWLEDGMENTS ★

THANK YOU TO AMERICA AND my fellow American citizens for my freedom. Thank you for giving me the abundance of opportunity to fulfill my dreams. So many kind Americans went out of their way to help me when I arrived in America. Goodness and moral integrity are the foundation upon which America was built, and this is what makes America unique around the world. In America, it is normal to be good, look out for neighbors, and help others who are in need. This is what makes America a light on the hill for others. My chance to live as a free man is only possible because of these ideals for which the founding fathers of America fought for and that have been carried forward to this day by Americans. I owe everything to America and the great people who go out of their way to give a hand up to those in need, doing what they can to help others realize their own American dream.

I would like to thank the one person without whom this book would never happen, my beautiful wife, Rachel Dzieran. She is more than my soul mate; she has never given up on me and is blessed with patience beyond understanding to help me find my best self. It is so important to me to share my story with the most accuracy possible that the stress can sometimes be overwhelming. Rachel's calm in my storms helped to keep my focus on completing this mission. I love you with all of my heart, thank you.

Another very important person to thank is Dan Bongino. Without Dan, this book would not be published and available for others to read and learn from. Thank you, Dan, for standing up for what is right and never backing down from a fight. Your relentless pursuit of truth is a benefit for everyone.

Thank you to the SEAL Teams and my teammates who taught me how to trust in others, their friendship, comradery, and for testing me every day. It was an honor to serve side by side with these men who sacrifice so much to keep our country and freedom safe.

A special thank you to fellow SEALs:

Thank you, Jocko Willink, for your SEAL Team leadership and for setting an example. You made me a better operator with your mentorship. Your investment in my story on your podcast contributed significantly to gaining broader interest in learning more and moving the book forward to where it is now.

Thank you, Rob O'Neil, Tej Gill, Dan Cerrillo, Ron Montgomery, Nicky Baggett, Tom Bostic, Chris Stroup, Duke Harbin, Kevin Kent, Mike Moriarty, Tony Gehl, Jared Ogden, Nicholas Olson, Chris Freisenbruch, Don Shipley, Marcus Luttrell, and so many more of my fellow SEAL brothers for your steadfast friendship on and off the battlefield.

Thank you to the other instrumental leaders in the Teams who contributed greatly to my growth as a Navy SEAL.

My gratitude to the Polish Special Forces (GROM) for excellence and expertise in conducting the joint Direct Action missions. Thank you for the cooperation, professionalism, and friendships. Special thanks to GROM Operators Pawel Manteńczuk, Grzegorz, Maniek, Tylut, Michał, Wronka,

Maniek, Janek, Bisu, Stary, Naval, Shagi, Poziomka, Damian, Kaśka, Żuku, Ousi, Dareek, and Kamel.

Thank you to Polish Solidarity leadership and my fellow political prisoners for your strength and resilience during dark days. Your passion in fighting for what is right, putting your personal safety at risk for innocents you would never meet, was and remains inspirational to me. Sincere thank you to Andrzej Krasuski, Edward Kędziorski, Jerzy Kaniewski, Krzysztof Bińkowski, Witold Kaszuba, Jerzy Kropiwnicki, Marek Kulczyk, Adam Pawluś, Dariusz Żytnicki, Marek Łada, Mirosław Cop, Roman Bielański, Leszek Tarasiuk, Jerzy Szyiński, Arkadiusz Czerwiński, Father Tadeusz Pajurek, and thousands of other political prisoners fighting Socialist oppression.

Everything I have, everything I own, I owe to America. Now I have a wonderful family, and everything I need to live, and most important—I am a free man. I live in the country of the free and brave, and I'm proud to be part of it. Please know that I am just an American—there is no hyphen on this American. I am a proud American.

DRAGO DZIERAN IS AN AMERICAN, retired U.S. Navy SEAL. He was born in Poland while it was under Communist rule and later spent time in a Communist prison as a political prisoner for his activism against the Socialist oppression. In Poland, political prisons or internment camps where political prisoners were held were often referred to as "gulags" in reference to the Soviet Union prison system and labor camps where they kept political prisoners.

Drago immigrated to the United States in 1984, and became a U.S. citizen in 1991. He arrived without knowing the language or customs but was thankful for the opportunities that awaited. When he became a United States citizen, he felt it was his moral obligation to serve his new country in the best capacity he could, and joined the military in support of the first Persian Gulf War. He enlisted in the Navy in 1991. After a twenty-year career as a Navy SEAL, Drago was granted an honorable discharge and retirement from the U.S. Navy in June 2011.

Drago's skills and certifications include Naval Special Warfare (NSW) Lead Breacher, NSW Instructor, Military Freefall Parachutist, Diving Supervisor, HRST Master, and Range Safety Officer. He is an expert and trainer in small arms, demolition, close-quarters combat, and explosives breaching. His expertise and training include HALO and HAHO, parachute rigger, and master naval parachutist.

During his Navy career, Drago was a member of SEAL Team Two, SEAL Team Four, and a BUD/S instructor at the Naval Special Warfare (NSW) Center in Coronado, California. His expertise was as a NSW Lead Breacher, and while deployed to Iraq in 2003, 2004, and 2005, he performed over one hundred combat Direct Action missions, and developed new breaching methods and a specialized breaching charge that minimized fragmentation, reducing potential injuries to non-combatants on target. This breaching charge allowed SEAL assault elements a smaller stand-off distance from the explosive breach and became widely used by SEALs throughout Iraq, saving many non-combatants' lives.

Drago was awarded the Bronze Star Medal with "V" Device for Valor, the Navy Commendation Medal with "V" Device for Valor, and the Army Commendation Medal, along with other awards and decorations. Following his honorable retirement after twenty years in the Navy, he began a successful career as a software engineer.

In 2009, Drago and his wife, Rachel, established the Navy SEALs Fund, a 501c3 nonprofit organization that provides support to all generations of UDT/Navy SEALs—former, retired, active duty—their immediate family members, and Gold Star families. Drago was inspired to open the charity after witnessing too many fellow SEAL teammates suffer severe injuries during combat and who were then left with no future. The Navy SEALs Fund is run by Navy SEALs and has no paid positions; no one receives a salary, nor other compensations or financial incentives. It is an honor to be able to give back and ensure no one goes it alone (www.navysealsfund.org).

Similarly to how Drago battled misinformation in Poland, he founded a freedom-of-speech platform that gives voice to all Americans without worry of censorship or Socialist fact-checkers: www.connectzing.com. ConnectZing will never give voice to America's enemies, nor allow for colluding against American values. ConnectZing is a place to speak freely, share ideas, agree, and even disagree with each other. You will not be cancelled for going against a certain political ideology or standing up against relative morality.

Drago is committed to encouraging others to get involved, stand up, and fight to preserve freedom and liberty in America. Every person has a voice, and every voice matters in America. His focus, as it has been since the first day he landed in America, is to simply be a better American today than yesterday, and to be a better American tomorrow than today. This is his Pledge to America.